DOOR OF HOPE

DOOR OF HOPE

A Century of the Bahá'í Faith in the Holy Land

David S. Ruhe

And I will give her . . . the valley of Achor
for a door of hope: and she shall sing there, as
in the days of her youth. . .

Hosea 2.15

GEORGE RONALD
OXFORD

GEORGE RONALD, Publisher
46 High Street, Kidlington, Oxford, OX5 2DN

ISBN 0–85398–149–3 (cased)
ISBN 0–85398–150–7 (paper)

Printed in England by Billing & Sons Ltd., Worcester

CONTENTS

Introduction

'Akká

The 'Akká Area

Haifa

Appendices

Preface and Acknowledgements

THE OBSERVANCES in 1968 which commemorated the centenary of Bahá'u'lláh's voyage on the Mediterranean Sea to His final exile and imprisonment in the Holy Land provided a befitting occasion for the publication of a book entitled *Bahá'í Holy Places at the World Centre*. It was compiled from mimeographed sheets prepared for the information of Bahá'í pilgrims visiting these Holy Places, but contained additional material and was augmented by a number of photographs. The present work is much expanded in content and detail, although the scope and arrangement of subject matter are much the same, while photographs and illustrations have been multiplied; it thus provides far greater information about important events, whether Bahá'í or others, associated with these holy sites. Since this book is conceived primarily as a service to Bahá'í pilgrims, it is place-related and does not follow a strict chronology, its narrative necessarily moving forwards and backwards in time as the place of drama changes. In the years since that first publication there has been an outpouring of new information on the history of the Bahá'í Faith, including the books by the Hand of the Cause Hasan M. Balyuzi and that of his associate Dr Moojan Momen, to which reference is frequently made. The many quotations from the rich materials available in familiar sources should, it is hoped, lead to the rereading of *God Passes By, Memorials of the Faithful, The Chosen Highway*, and other important volumes on the formative days of the Faith.

Comment should be made on sources of information apart from those listed in the Bibliography. The Bahá'í World Centre collection of original Tablets, letters and documents concerning the affairs of the Bahá'í Faith is very extensive. Slowly many important data are coming to light, including information from the Founders of the Faith and from Their contemporaries. Simultaneously, the increased interest of

1

Jewish and Christian scholars in Biblical archaeology and history has generated a number of significant studies of ancient 'Akká, Haifa, and their environs, and has made it possible to achieve new perspectives. It seems probable that another decade will see illuminating work which will further expand our understanding of the development of the Bahá'í Faith in the Holy Land.

In the uncovering of new information and the mustering of old data, particular thanks are due to Mr Ṣaláḥ al-Dín Jarráḥ. The Research Department of the World Centre has kindly supplied material when asked, including new translations of a number of passages. In particular, Dr Vaḥíd Ra'fatí has generously assisted with these translations and in checking the transliteration of Arabic and Persian words. Hebrew names have come from the commonly accepted local maps and guidebooks. The assistance of Engineer Bernard Dichter, whose love of 'Akká has made him a collector of many forms of data concerning the prison city, is warmly acknowledged; indeed, he has volunteered much of the important new substance of this book. For archaeological data Dr Ze'ev Goldmann, former Curator of the 'Akká Municipal Museum and supervisor of the first Hospitaller fortress excavations under the barracks and elsewhere, and Dr Moshe Dotan, Professor of Archaeology at the Haifa University and director of the ongoing dig on Tell 'Akká, have supplied valuable new details from their investigations. To Father Elias Friedman, OCD, an accolade for his exhaustive studies on the caves of Elijah and the Christian history of Mount Carmel, and gratitude for his willing advice. In the quest for accuracy Dr Moojan Momen and Mr Ian Semple have been sharp critics of the text. In its careful editing Mrs Marion Hofman has shown her deep knowledge of the Faith, without which the text would have been studded with errors large and small. A debt of gratitude is due to Mrs Lorana Kerfoot for accepting the onerous task of typing a constantly changing manuscript, and to Mrs Wendi Momen for her detailed and most useful index.

The photographs derive in the main from the archival collection of the Audio-Visual Department of the World Centre, and from new pictures taken by Messrs Lacey Crawford and Tom Thompson, to whom great credit is due for their exacting labours in producing the best possible prints from originals which often were seriously damaged. Photographs in this collection which were made available in 1909 by Dr Edward Getsinger (probably taken *circa* 1900), and others taken by Mr Clarence L. Welsh (1921), Miss Effie Baker (1925–37), and Dr Luṭfu'lláh Ḥakím (1920 *et seq.*) deserve special mention. Dr Alex Carmel, Professor of History at Haifa University, has provided valuable pictures from his collection. Several nineteenth-century illustrations have been taken from the book of essays by Mr Laurence Oliphant, edited by Mr Rechavam Ze'evy. The drawings have been executed by Mrs Audrey Marcus and by the author. This rich selection of photographs and drawings has been chosen to orient the Bahá'í pilgrim and strengthen his experiences.

Historically, the Holy Land has exercised an influence upon human affairs out of all proportion to its diminutive size, and without doubt it will continue to do so in the future. To 'Akká, 'the silver city', Mount Carmel, the 'mountain of God', and their environs come ever-increasing streams of Bahá'í pilgrims and visitors seeking their spiritual and administrative home. It is hoped that this book will be of particular use and interest to them, to answer the questions of the curious, to enrich pilgrim days, to provoke wide reading of original sources, and to be a perennial reference on this 'most Holy Land'.

DAVID S. RUHE

Haifa
September 1982

3

Introduction

1   The Holy Land

IN ISRAEL, the Holy Land of Jews, Christians, Muslims and Bahá'ís, Bahá'í pilgrims find themselves in the midst of a dense concentration of meaningful sites of a shared and progressive spiritual evolution. How vital to the promised consummation of that evolution is

. . . the Holy Land – the Land promised by God to Abraham, sanctified by the Revelation of Moses, honoured by the lives and labours of the Hebrew patriarchs, judges, kings and prophets, revered as the cradle of Christianity, and as the place where Zoroaster, according to 'Abdu'l-Bahá's testimony, had 'held converse with some of the Prophets of Israel', and associated by Islám with the Apostle's night-journey, through the seven heavens, to the throne of the Almighty. Within the confines of this holy and enviable country, 'the nest of all the Prophets of God', 'the Vale of God's unsearchable Decree, the snow-white Spot, the Land of unfading splendour' was the Exile of Baghdád, of Constantinople and Adrianople condemned to spend no less than a third of the allotted span of His life, and over half of the total period of His Mission. 'It is difficult', declares 'Abdu'l-Bahá, 'to understand how Bahá'u'lláh could have been obliged to leave Persia, and to pitch His tent in this Holy Land, but for the persecution of His enemies, His banishment and exile.'

Indeed such a consummation, He assures us, had been actually prophesied 'through the tongue of the Prophets two or three thousand years before'. God, 'faithful to His promise,' had, 'to some of the Prophets' 'revealed and given the good news that the Lord of Hosts should be manifested in the Holy Land.' Isaiah had, in this connection, announced in his Book: 'Get thee up into the high mountain, O Zion that bringest good tidings; lift up thy voice with strength, O Jerusalem, that bringest good tidings. Lift it up, be not afraid; say unto the cities of Judah: "Behold your God! Behold the Lord God will come with strong hand, and His arm shall rule for Him."' David, in his Psalms, had predicted: 'Lift up your heads, O ye gates; even lift them up, ye everlasting doors – and the King of Glory shall come in. Who is this King of Glory? The Lord of Hosts, He is the King of Glory.' 'Out of Zion, the perfection of beauty, God hath shined. Our God shall come, and shall not keep silence.' Amos had, likewise, foretold His coming: 'The Lord will roar from Zion, and utter His voice from Jerusalem; and the habitations of the shepherds shall mourn, and the top of Carmel shall wither.' (*God Passes By*, pp. 183–4)

The fulfilment of prophecies can be realized in visiting the authentic places mentioned in the Holy Books, places invested with singularly vital significances. A pilgrimage to Israel constitutes a journey in progressive Revelation, an experience confirming the reality of the concept of evolution in religion.

The entire land recalls the ancient coming of the Hebrews, their return from captivity in Egypt in about the thirteenth century BC and their establishment of a culture based on religion, stemming from Moses and the prophets. The 'Akká area Jacob and Joshua assigned to the Tribe of Asher,[1] and the Haifa area to the Tribe of Zebulon.[2] Close together in the tiny country of Israel are the four holy cities of Judaism: Jerusalem and Hebron, Tiberias and Safed. Archaeological exposure of the ancient cities and historic places has refreshed the reality of the Torah and the other Jewish books called the Old Testament by Christians. The present-day Israel of the Return of the Jews amply demonstrates the fulfilment of prophecy and also the development of the land.

The Ministry of Jesus the Christ can be felt in His Galilean neighbourhood and along the Jordan Valley. From Nazareth to Tabor and Na'im, from Cana to Capernaum and the Mount of the Beatitudes, from Bethsaida to Khorazín, Tabgha, Kursí and Migdala the trail of His teachings and life can be followed. At Bethlehem there is the place of His birth, near Jericho the Judean wilderness and the Mount of Temptation, on the Jordan River the place of the baptism by John, in Jerusalem the tragic place of His crucifixion. Indeed, the compass of the land is so small that in mere hours one can relive the significant events of Jesus' three years of teaching and sacrifice.

In Jerusalem, on Mount Moriah outside David's city at the traditional site of Abraham's averted sacrifice of his son, where had stood the first and second Temples of the Jews, there now are two mosques of Islám. One, al-Aqṣá, 'the farthest point', in its name commemorates Muḥammad's vision of His night ascent to heaven,[3] while the second, the Dome of the Rock (built by 'Abd-al-Malik in AD 691), is erected over Abraham's rock from which, in the dream, sprang Muḥammad's visionary steed al-Buráq.

8

In the Haifa–'Akká area the Bahá'í Holy Places include a number of places large and small, developed or to be developed, which have been hallowed by the Dust of the Forerunner and by twenty-four years of Revelation of the Supreme Prophet, have witnessed fifty-three years of devoted service and teaching by the Master, 'Abdu'l-Bahá, and bear the imprint of a lifetime of selfless and indefatigable labour by the Guardian.

2   The Banishments of Bahá'u'lláh

WHEN IN 1852 Bahá'u'lláh was spared a martyr's death in Ţihrán, He was banished for life from His native land, and chose 'Iráq as His new home. The Guardian of the Bahá'í Faith, Shoghi Effendi, relates the profound import of this event.

The Sháh's edict, equivalent to an order for the immediate expulsion of Bahá'u'lláh from Persian territory, opens a new and glorious chapter in the history of the first Bahá'í century . . . The process which it set in motion . . . carried Him as far as the shores of the Holy Land, thereby fulfilling the prophecies recorded in both the Old and the New Testaments, redeeming the pledge enshrined in various traditions attributed to the Apostle of God and the Imáms who succeeded Him, and ushering in the long-awaited restoration of Israel to the ancient cradle of its Faith . . .

This enforced and hurried departure of Bahá'u'lláh from His native land, accompanied by some of His relatives, recalls in some of its aspects, the precipitate flight of the Holy Family into Egypt; the sudden migration of Muḥammad, soon after His assumption of the prophetic office, from Mecca to Medina; the exodus of Moses, His brother and His followers from the land of their birth, in response to the Divine summons, and above all the banishment of Abraham from Ur of the Chaldees to the Promised Land – a banishment which, in the multitudinous benefits it conferred upon so many divers peoples, faiths and nations, constitutes the nearest historical approach to the incalculable blessings destined to be vouchsafed, in this day, and in future ages, to the whole human race, in direct consequence of the exile suffered by Him Whose Cause is the flower and fruit of all previous Revelations.

'Abdu'l-Bahá, after enumerating in His *Some Answered Questions* the far-reaching consequences of Abraham's banishment, significantly affirms that 'since the exile of Abraham from Ur to Aleppo in Syria produced this result, we must consider what will be the effect of the exile of Bahá'u'lláh in His several removes from Ṭihrán to Baghdád, from thence to Constantinople, to Rumelia [Adrianople] and to the Holy Land'. (*God Passes By*, pp. 106–8)

In a further commentary on the meaning of the exile of Bahá'u'lláh, Shoghi Effendi stated that in Adrianople

. . . an indestructible Faith . . . reached its meridian glory through the proclamation of the Mission of Bahá'u'lláh to the kings, the rulers and ecclesiastical leaders of the world in both the East and the West. Close on the heels of this unprecedented victory had followed the climax of His sufferings, a banishment to the penal colony of 'Akká, decreed by Sulṭán 'Abdu'l-'Azíz. This had been hailed by vigilant enemies as the signal for the final extermination of a much feared and hated adversary, and it had heaped upon that Faith in this fortress-town, designated by Bahá'u'lláh as His 'Most Great Prison', calamities from both within and without, such as it had never before experienced. (ibid. p. 404)

The banishment, lasting no less than twenty-four years, to which two Oriental despots had, in their implacable enmity and short-sightedness, combined to condemn Bahá'u'lláh, will go down in history as a period which witnessed a miraculous and truly revolutionizing change in the circumstances attending the life and

activities of the Exile Himself, will be chiefly remembered for the widespread recrudescence of persecution, intermittent but singularly cruel, throughout His native country and the simultaneous increase in the number of His followers, and, lastly, for an enormous extension in the range and volume of His writings. (ibid. p. 185)

The events in Adrianople which precipitated the final exile of Bahá'u'lláh to 'Akká, came to a climax in 1868. To satisfy the importunities of the Persian officials in Constantinople and the suspicions of the Turkish authorities

The fateful decision was eventually arrived at to banish Bahá'u'lláh to the penal colony of 'Akká . . .

On the morning of the 2nd of Jamádíyu'l-Avval 1285 AH (21 August 1868) they all embarked [at Gallipoli] in an Austrian-Lloyd steamer for Alexandria, touching at Madellí, and stopping for two days at Smyrna, where Jináb-i-Munír, surnamed Ismu'lláhu'l-Muníb, became gravely ill, and had, to his great distress, to be left behind in a hospital where he soon after died. In Alexandria they transhipped into a steamer of the same company, bound for Haifa, where, after brief stops at Port Said and Jaffa, they landed, setting out, a few hours later, in a sailing vessel, for 'Akká, where they disembarked, in the course of the afternoon of the 12th of Jamádíyu'l-Avval 1285 AH (31 August 1868). (ibid. pp. 179, 182)

The arrival of Bahá'u'lláh in 'Akká marks the opening of the last phase of His forty-year-long ministry, the final stage, and indeed the climax, of the banishment in which the whole of that ministry was spent. (ibid. p. 183)

Nineteenth-century drawing of 'Akká from the beach to the south. The minaret of the Mosque of al-Jazzár and the dark citadel are prominent on the skyline. (Oliphant, *Haifa*)

3 Stages of Bahá'u'lláh's Journey to and Sojourn in the Holy Land

The journey of Bahá'u'lláh and His
companions from Gallipoli to Haifa lasted
from 21 August 1868 to 31 August 1868 — 11 days

Bahá'u'lláh and His party were transferred
from the steamer which carried them to Haifa
to a sailing vessel which arrived in 'Akká
during the afternoon of 31 August 1868. The
time spent in Haifa was — A few hours

The buildings and houses occupied by
Bahá'u'lláh during His life in the Holy
Land were as follows:

1. The Barracks, 'Akká — 2 years, 2 months and 5 days
   (31 August 1868 to 4 November 1870)

2. The Houses of Malik, Khavvám
   and Rábi'ih★ — About 10 months

3. The House of 'Údí Khammár and

4. The House of 'Abbúd★ — Approximately 5 years and 9 months
   (September 1871 to June 1877)

5. The Riḍván Garden — Occasional visits

6. The Mansion of Mazra'ih — Approximately 2 years and 4 months
   (June 1877 to September 1879)

7. The Mansion of Bahjí — Approximately 12 years and 9 months
   (September 1879 to 29 May 1892)†

The total period of the sojourn of Bahá'u'lláh in the Holy Land was
23 years, 8 months and 29 (or 30) days, from 31 August 1868 to 29
May 1892.

★From the Prison, Bahá'u'lláh was transferred directly to the House of Malik, thence to the
Houses of Khavvám and Rábi'ih and finally to the Houses of 'Údí Khammár and 'Abbúd. The
Bahá'ís own and visit only what is called the House of 'Abbúd, the most important of them,
which now incorporates the House of 'Údí Khammár.
†Towards the end of the period in the Mansion of Bahjí, Bahá'u'lláh visited Haifa three times,
in August 1883, in April 1890, and in the summer of 1891 for about three months.

4 Pilgrimage to the Holy Land

PILGRIMAGES TO the Holy Places associated with a faith are a common practice in the organized religions of mankind. In the Bahá'í Faith such pilgrimage is both a privilege and an obligation, for in the *Kitáb-i-Aqdas*

Bahá'u'lláh specifically ordains pilgrimage to the Most Great House in Baghdád and to the House of the Báb in Shíráz . . . In a Tablet to an individual believer 'Abdu'l-Bahá commented on the general subject of visits to holy places: 'You have asked about visiting holy places and the observance of marked reverence towards these resplendent spots. Holy places are undoubtedly centres of the outpouring of Divine grace, because on entering the illumined sites associated with martyrs and holy souls, and by observing reverence, both physical and spiritual, one's heart is moved with great tenderness. But there is no obligation for everyone to visit such places, other than the three, namely: the Most Holy Shrine,[1] the Blessed House in Baghdád and the venerated House of the Báb in Shíráz. To visit these is obligatory if one can afford it and is able to do so, and if no obstacle stands in one's way . . . These three Holy Places are consecrated to pilgrimage . . .' (*Synopsis and Codification*, p. 61)

After Bahá'u'lláh made His formal Proclamation in Adrianople in 1867, the custom of making pilgrimages began through His revelation of two Tablets of Pilgrimage relating to the Houses in Baghdád and Shíráz. Also,

. . . it was during that period that the first pilgrimages were made to the residence of One Who was now the visible Centre of a newly-established Faith – pilgrimages which by reason of their number and nature an alarmed government in Persia was first impelled to restrict, and later to prohibit, but which were the precursors of the converging streams of pilgrims who, from East and West, at first under perilous and arduous circumstances, were to direct their steps towards the prison-fortress of 'Akká . . . (*God Passes By*, p. 177)

Over the course of more than a century since the beginning

13

of Bahá'í pilgrimages to the Holy Land, great changes have taken place, not only in the access to the many Holy Places hallowed through association with Bahá'u'lláh and 'Abdu'l-Bahá, but also in

. . . the marked improvement in the conditions surrounding the pilgrimages performed by its devoted adherents to its consecrated shrines at its world centre – pilgrimages originally arduous, perilous, tediously long, often made on foot, at times ending in disappointment, and confined to a handful of harassed Oriental followers, gradually attracting, under steadily improving circumstances of security and comfort, an ever swelling number of new converts converging from the four corners of the globe . . . (ibid. xvii)

It is proper to expect that, with the spread of the Cause throughout the world and its increasing membership, the corresponding development of the World Centre will produce a great expansion of the pilgrimage experience. Just as the 'flow of pilgrims . . . constitutes the life-blood' of that Centre, so the World Centre itself, which is the spiritual heart, is growing larger and stronger as it beats the pulse of the new Bahá'í society.

Mount Carmel and Haifa, south-westward view from the beach of the Bay of Haifa, long used as the highway between Haifa and 'Akká. (Welsh, 1921)

ʻAkká

5 'Akká, Museum City of Northern Israel

TRULY TO APPRECIATE the present 'museum city' of 'Akká one must glimpse its more than 4000-year-long history, for what one may visit inside the formidable walls is at most only the last four layers of the city, the visible topmost living one being the Arab–Turkish city of Fakhri'd-Dín, Záhiru'l-'Umar (Daher-el-Omar), Aḥmad al-Jazzár and their successors, the invisible three being those of the Crusaders, the Arabs, and the Byzantines. However, there is another 'Akká: that of thirteen or more earlier cities dating from before Biblical Akko up through Hellenic and Roman Ptolemais, whose remnants lie under the earth of the tell to the east of the present-day city. There they comprise the layers of a knoll which in more recent times has variously been called the Hill of the Shards (Tell al-Fakhkhár), Napoleon's Hill, and Hill of Richard the Lion-Heart, and is accurately known as Tell 'Akká. Methodical archaeological work on the tell by the University of Haifa began in 1973, and has revealed much more of the troubled history of this city of the Canaanites, Hyksos, sea peoples, and Phoenicians. The city flowered during the Persian and Greek periods, reaching its greatest commercial prosperity under Greek rule and sheltering in Roman times an eastern suburb for the invalided veterans of four legions under the name Colonia Claudio Felix Ptolemais.

Not a small thing even in terms of the tell's eventful history of more than 2,500 years before its quiescence after the Arab conquest, Bahá'u'lláh twice pitched His tent at the ancient tell during His days of sojourn at Bahjí.

It seems likely that the expansion from a small walled city on the mound near the bay to become the much larger city, embracing the nearby rocky ridge and peninsula at the sea, occurred during its Persian and Hellenic periods (sixth to first centuries BC), when latterly it was called Ptolemais, after

Nineteenth-century 'Akká port from the south, as Bahá'u'lláh and His fellow exiles would have seen it on that momentous day of their arrival in August 1868.

17

Ptolemy II Philadelphus. The rulers of those times saw the advantages of port facilities in the shelter of the peninsula, as did the Roman and Arab conquerors who succeeded them. Later, after its capture by the Crusaders in 1104, the city was heavily fortified, a wall and moat constructed across the top of the peninsula to form a very defensible land line. As Sanuto's medieval map shows, the northern and eastern fortifications enclosed perhaps 80 acres, while a northern walled salient, angled to the coast above, enclosed a large added area called the Mount Musard Quarter; the Crusader city was thus approximately double that of the 62 acres of the present walled town.

After the fall of Jerusalem to the Seljuk commander Saladin (Ṣaláḥ al-Dín) and thereafter his defeat of the Crusaders at the Horns of Hittin near Tiberias, Accon (as it was then named) was taken by the Muslims in 1187. It was retaken by the Christians in 1191 and, since Jerusalem was still held by the Ayyúbids, was made the capital of the Kingdom of Jerusalem for the next hundred years, when the town reached its highest development. During that century the *castellum* of the Crusader kings, and the great interior forts of the military orders of the Knights of the Hospital and the Knights of the Temple were extended and strengthened. To the fortified quarters of the merchants from the Italian city-states of Pisa, Genoa and

'Akká city from its southern beach approach (Welsh, 1921)

Venice were added city sections assigned to the trader-colonists from Marseilles, Amalfi, Florence, Lucca and Ancona, and also sections assigned to the new military order of the Teutonic Knights, to the knights of England, and not least to the Holy See for its Patriarchate-Archbishopric of Jerusalem in the Santa Crux section.

The Crusades witnessed the visits of many kings, warriors and churchmen, but there were others more important to the progress of mankind. The greatest physician and rabbi of the Middle Ages, the Spanish-born Moshe ben Maimon, or Maimonides (the Rambam), visited Acre for some months during his last year of life, dying and being buried in Tiberias in 1204. St. Francis of Assisi came to Acre in 1218, remaining in the Holy Land for several months, and there establishing the first Franciscan monastery of the Levant. In 1271 Marco Polo passed through en route to Cathay, a Venetian youth travelling with his uncle Maffeo.

In 1291 the Mamelukes commanded by al-Malik al-Ashraf stormed the city, burned and destroyed it. The fall of the city was decisive, the climactic end of the bloody and ill-conceived dream of the Crusaders, for very soon what remained of the forces of Christendom withdrew from the Holy Land and from the entire Middle East.

The city was of no significance until French merchants built the K͟hán-i -Afranj in the early sixteenth century. Then during a brief period from 1595 onward the Druze emir of Sidon, Fak͟hri'd-Dín, built a customs house, mosque and palace, and undertook some reconstruction of the Hospitaller complex. In the mid-eighteenth century the Galilean Beduin chieftain, Z̧áhiru'l-'Umar, made 'Akká his centre of power, from 1749 carving out a semi-independent pashalik near the outer edge of the decadent Ottoman Empire. Shrewd enough not to rebel from the Sublime Porte, for defection would soon invite a retributive Turkish army, he negotiated a semi-autonomous relationship with the Sultan, then set about rebuilding 'Akká as his capital and centre of trade, while simultaneously developing a small walled port city called Haifa across the bay at a site east of ancient Haifa. He reconstructed the fortifications of 'Akká, whose northern inner walls and moat seen in the present city are of his building.

Upon 'Umar's murder in August 1775 the Albanian mercenary captain Aḥmad of Beirut was named Páshá of Sidon. He immediately moved to 'Akká and quickly earned his title al-Jazzár, the Butcher, by ruthlessly eliminating his opposition, thereafter rapidly consolidating his authority from Beirut to Caesarea and eastward to the territory of the Governor of Damascus. During his rule from 1775 to 1804 al-Jazzár built the mosque carrying his name upon foundations of the Crusader church of St. John, erected two k͟háns or inns, constructed the public bath at the south side of the citadel, occupied the Governorate of Fak͟hri'd-Dín and 'Umar over the Hospitallers' hospital section, built an extensive market later destroyed by an explosion and fire, constructed the first aqueduct to the springs of Kabrí which Napoleon promptly ruined, and greatly strengthened 'Umar's fortifications by adding new walls and a deep dry moat. With the aid of a British fleet under Sir Sidney Smith, and local plagues in the French camp, he successfully repelled the attack of Napoleon's small expeditionary army and fleet in June 1799, thus ending one chapter of French ambition for Middle Eastern dominion.

Early in the nineteenth century Sulaymán Páshá (1805–19) further extended the fortifications and strengthened the citadel, rebuilt the White Souk (As-Súq al-Abyaḍ), and began a new aqueduct to the springs of Kabrí along its present lines. In 1819 'Abdu'lláh Páshá succeeded him, and further fortified the city, augmenting the square tower of the citadel, only to fall victim

Bahá'ís standing near the site where Bahá'u'lláh pitched His tent at the base of Tell 'Akká. In the distance (left) can be seen the Mansion of Bahjí. (Getsinger, c. 1900)

20

to the ambitions of Muḥammad-'Alí Pás<u>h</u>á, governor of Egypt, whose capable son Ibráhím Bey shelled and conquered the city in 1831–2. Ibráhím Bey was driven out in his turn by the very destructive bombardment of a British–Turkish–Austrian fleet under Stopford and Napier in 1840. By mid-century the severely damaged city of 'Akká had reached the nadir of its decline, losing the dominance of the western Galilee. It was during this period of decadence and depopulation, not only for the city but for the entire area, that Bahá'u'lláh and His company of exiles were transported to the Turkish 'Bastille of the East' which then, thanks to economic disruptions and endemic diseases, appears to have been occupied by fewer than 10,000 dispirited persons.

A succession of pás<u>h</u>ás of variable qualities governed or misgoverned the prison-city. 'Akká's chronic malaise grew irreparable even as Haifa, across the bay, began to achieve commercial dominance of the region. During the British Mandate, the citadel and barracks became the hated central prison of the country, the town thus earning a new measure of dislike. By 1948, with the coming of the State of Israel and its conquest by Israeli forces, 'Akká had become a small port serving a few shallow-draught fishing vessels. Yet, by the time of the Yom Kippur War in 1973 it was plain, from the northward spread of burgeoning Haifa and with new Jewish 'Akko spreading out on the flanks of the old city, that the prophetic vision of 'Abdu'l-Bahá soon would be realized: the two cities would fuse into one metropolis of the greatest significance in that Day of Peace expected by the Prophets. In short, 'Akká's future is daily growing brighter, now as a museum city within the walls and as an industrial centre of northern Israel outside them, but also, it must be added, as an emergent holy city of the Bahá'í Faith.

6 The Prison City

'Akká am I, splendour of the country,
Full of grace, and of blessing without end,
Mounts Carmel and Lebanon surround me,
Where God's Majesty is revealed.
Holy is my land from time immemorial,
Close, so close am I to Godhead immanent.

Alkharizi

FOUR THOUSAND YEARS ago the city now called 'Akká was a pre-Hyksos town named Accho, a stronghold of the proto-Canaanitic ancient coastal peoples. In later centuries it was impregnable to the attacks of the Israelite tribe of Asher which had been allocated the western Galilee as its domain, nor was it conquered by the warrior kings of Israel but was only infiltrated by their people.[1] The city was then situated on the hillock now called the Tell[2] of 'Akká, to the east of the present walled town, and was the best port below Beirut and Tyre on the entire reach of sea-coast to the Nile delta, serving as the centre of sea trade for the Galilee and for the Hauran to the east. Despite its not being an Israelite city, it accumulated an oddly significant Scriptural history which is succinctly summarized in *God Passes By*:

'Akká, the 'metropolis of the owl'. This earliest aerial photograph of the prison city shows the barrack-square at the upper right and the original port area lower right with the remnants of the Crusader–Turkish breakwater. (Adolf Kärcher 1914)

'Akká, itself, flanked by the 'glory of Lebanon', and lying in full view of the 'splendour of Carmel', at the foot of the hills which enclose the home of Jesus Christ Himself, had been described by David as 'the Strong City', designated by Hosea as 'a door of hope', and alluded to by Ezekiel as 'the gate that looketh towards the East', whereunto 'the glory of the God of Israel came from the way of the East', His voice 'like a noise of many waters'. To it the Arabian Prophet had referred as 'a city in Syria to which God hath shown His special mercy', situated 'betwixt two mountains . . . in the middle of a meadow', 'by the shore of the sea . . . suspended beneath the Throne', 'white, whose whiteness is pleasing unto God'. 'Blessed the man', He, moreover, as confirmed by Bahá'u'lláh, had declared, 'that hath visited 'Akká, and blessed he that hath visited the visitor of 'Akká'. Furthermore, 'He that raiseth therein the call to prayer, his voice will be lifted up unto Paradise.' And again: 'The poor of 'Akká are the kings of Paradise and the princes thereof. A month in 'Akká is better than a thousand years elsewhere.' Moreover, in a remarkable tradition, which is contained in <u>Sh</u>ay<u>kh</u> Ibnu'l-'Arabí's work, entitled *Futúhát-i-Makkíyyih*, and which is recognized as an authentic utterance of Muḥammad, and is quoted by Mírzá Abu'l-Faḍl in his *Fará'id*, this significant prediction has been made: 'All of them [the companions of the Qá'im] shall be slain except One Who shall reach the plain of 'Akká, the Banquet-Hall of God.' (p. 184)

The city's early Canaanite–Phoenician centuries are now being systematically investigated, while later events are historically well documented. Among the earliest established events is the conquest of Accho by the Persians in the sixth century BC. Then in 331 BC Alexander the Great swept through the land, and later the city was renamed Ptolemais after Ptolemy II Philadelphus, son of one of his generals, the name also reflecting the Hellenization of the country by the Greek conquerors.

The city expanded further under pagan Rome[3] and Christian Byzantium, spreading from the hill to the nearby peninsula. Besieged and taken by the Persians in AD 614, it was soon retaken by the Byzantines and finally conquered by the Arabs in AD 636. Reaching its apogee under the Crusaders in the twelfth and thirteenth centuries, it became the capital of the Crusader Kingdom of Jerusalem for a hundred years, only to be destroyed by the Mamelukes in 1291. During the next two-hundred-and-fifty years the city was largely a ruin, occupied by few people. Re-establishment of the port began with French merchants in the sixteenth century, and there was a further renascence under the Druze leader Fakhri'd-Dín. Massively rebuilt in the mid-eighteenth century by a ruler subservient to the Ottoman Turkish Empire, it suffered very damaging attacks by Napoleon in 1799, by the Egyptians in 1832, and the British in 1840, and was a city in radical decline at the coming of Bahá'u'lláh in 1868. By that time

'Akká, the ancient Ptolemais, the St. Jean d'Acre of the Crusaders, that had successfully defied the siege of Napoleon, had sunk, under the Turks, to the level of a penal colony to which murderers, highway robbers and political agitators were consigned from all parts of the Turkish empire. It was girt about by a double system of ramparts; was inhabited by a people whom Bahá'u'lláh stigmatized as 'the generation of vipers'; was devoid of any source of water within its gates; was flea-infested, damp and honey-combed with gloomy, filthy and tortuous lanes. 'According to what they say,' the Supreme Pen has recorded in the *Lawḥ-i-Sulṭán*, 'it is the most desolate of the cities of the world, the most unsightly of them in appearance, the most detestable in climate, and the foulest in water. It is as though it were the metropolis of the owl.' So putrid was its air that, according to a proverb, a bird when flying over it would drop dead. (*God Passes By*, pp. 185–6)

Bahá'u'lláh Himself, as attested by Nabíl in his narrative, had, as far back as the first years of His banishment to Adrianople, alluded to that same city in His *Lawḥ-i-Sayyáh*, designating it as the 'Vale of Nabíl', the word Nabíl being equal in numerical value to that of 'Akká. 'Upon Our arrival,' that Tablet had predicted, 'We were welcomed with banners of light, whereupon the Voice of the Spirit cried out saying: "Soon will all that dwell on earth be enlisted under these banners." ' (ibid. p. 184)

His arrival at the penal colony of 'Akká, far from proving the end of His afflictions, was but the beginning of a major crisis, character-

24

ized by bitter suffering, severe restrictions, and intense turmoil, which, in its gravity, surpassed even the agonies of the Síyáh-Chál of Ṭihrán, and to which no other event, in the history of the entire century can compare, except the internal convulsion that rocked the Faith in Adrianople. (ibid. p. 185)

'His enemies', 'Abdu'l-Bahá, referring to this same theme, has written, 'intended that His imprisonment should completely destroy and annihilate the blessed Cause, but this prison was, in reality, of the greatest assistance, and became the means of its development.' (ibid. p. 196)

Aerial view of 'Akká from the north, showing the northern moats, the citadel and barrack-square, the Mosque of al-Jazzár, the three khás, and, above left, the reconstructed breakwater and harbour, with the lighthouse at the far right. (1972)

7   The Arrival and the Barracks

THE ARRIVAL OF the exiled Bahá'ís in pestilential 'Akká occurred in the late afternoon of 31 August 1868. Poignantly the Greatest Holy Leaf, the daughter of Bahá'u'lláh, relates the circumstances of that hard day:

At length we arrived at Haifa, where we had to be carried ashore in chairs. Here we remained for a few hours. Now we embarked again for the last bit of our sea journey. The heat of that month of July [*sic*] was overpowering. We were put into a sailing boat. There being no wind, and no shelter from the burning rays of the sun, we spent eight hours of positive misery, and at last we had reached 'Akká, the end of our journey.

The landing at this place was achieved with much difficulty; the ladies of our party were carried ashore.

All the townspeople had assembled to see the arrival of the prisoners. Having been told that we were infidels, criminals, and sowers of sedition, the attitude of the crowd was threatening. Their yelling of curses and execrations filled us with fresh misery. We were terrified of the unknown! We knew not what the fate of our party, the friends and ourselves would be. (*The Chosen Highway*, p. 66)

The sea gate, interior (Ḥakím, early 1920s)

The passage into the city occurred through the sea gate, a narrow portal under the muzzles of the heavy cannon guarding the harbour mouth. The gate lay just south of the Khán-i-'Avámíd; of massive wood faced with overlapping band iron, it opened into a courtyard with stalls for merchandise. The party of 'exiles, men, women and children, were, under the eyes of a curious and callous population that had assembled at the port to behold the "God of the Persians" ' (*God Passes By*, p. 186), conducted through the city while bypassing the kháns (caravanserais), taken past the police station[1] and through the thronging market streets, past the White Súq and the Mosque of al-Jazzár until finally they came, uneasy and unhappy, to the walls of the barracks. Climbing the high stairs, they passed into the fortress prison through the eastern gateway. Inside the

The sea gate of 'Akká, at the southern edge of the port. Note the round cannon tower which protected the harbour and the bayside fortifications. The Khán-i-'Avámíd is at the right, its windows seen above the prow of the boat. (1920s)

The police station in the centre of 'Akká, where Bahá'u'lláh and the exile party briefly paused before proceeding to the prison. The old building, much altered, today serves as a coffee-house.

The eastern face of the barrack-square, with the stairway and gateway through which Bahá'u'lláh and the exiles first entered the prison. (Getsinger, c. 1900)

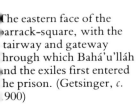

barracks they were taken to the north-western wing of the citadel, hot, bleak and forbidding, where sentinels were detailed to guard them. The Prophet Himself tells of those hours:

'The first night', Bahá'u'lláh testifies in the *Lawḥ-i-Ra'ís*, 'all were deprived of either food or drink . . . They even begged for water, and were refused.' So filthy and brackish was the water in the pool of the courtyard that no one could drink it. Three loaves of black and salty bread were assigned to each, which they were later permitted to exchange, when escorted by guards to the market, for two of better quality. Subsequently they were allowed a mere pittance as substitute for the allotted dole of bread. (*God Passes By*, p. 187)

Shoghi Effendi further describes those first grim weeks:

Explicit orders had been issued by the Sulṭán and his ministers to subject the exiles, who were accused of having grievously erred and led others far astray, to the strictest confinement. Hopes were confidently expressed that the sentence of life-long imprisonment pronounced against them would lead to their eventual extermination. The farmán of Sulṭán 'Abdu'l-'Azíz, dated the fifth of Rabí'u'th-Thání 1285 AH (26 July 1868), not only condemned them to perpetual banishment, but stipulated their strict incarceration, and forbade them to associate either with each other or with the local inhabitants. The text of the farmán itself was read publicly [on a Friday], soon after the arrival of the exiles, in the principal mosque of the city[2] as a warning to the population . . . (ibid. p. 186)

All fell sick, except two, shortly after their arrival. Malaria, dysentery, combined with the sultry heat, added to their miseries. Three succumbed, among them two brothers, who died the same night, 'locked', as testified by Bahá'u'lláh, 'in each other's arms'. The carpet used by Him He gave to be sold in order to provide for their winding-sheets and burial. The paltry sum obtained after it had been auctioned was delivered to the guards, who had refused to bury them without first being paid the necessary expenses. Later, it was learned that, unwashed and unshrouded, they had buried them, without coffins, in the clothes they wore, though, as affirmed by Bahá'u'lláh, they were given twice the amount required for their burial. 'None', He Himself has written, 'knoweth what befell Us, except God, the Almighty, the All-Knowing . . . From the foundation of the world until the present day a cruelty such as this hath neither been seen nor heard of.' 'He hath, during the greater part of His life,' He, referring to Himself, has, moreover, recorded, 'been sore-tried in the clutches of His enemies. His sufferings have now reached their culmination in this afflictive Prison, into which His oppressors have so unjustly thrown Him.' (ibid. p. 187)

The north-west building of the prison complex where Bahá'u'lláh and His family were confined (centre). Note the open court on the ground floor and the doorway, in deep shadow, leading to the inner stairway to the upper floor. The stone-blocked arches of the upper floor suggest that originally this level also had an open court. At the left are the arches of the former Khán of 'Alí Páshá. (Ḥakím, 1922)

The bleak and forbidding north-west corner of the barrack-square of the prison complex, to which Bahá'u'lláh and His fellow exiles were taken. Note the now unused fountain in the courtyard, foreground. (c. 1912)

Those first months in the prison were well-nigh intolerable, yet 'Abdu'l-Bahá then, as always, was the tireless servant of the sick, the needy, the disconsolate. But, towards the ending of autumn, the exiles' adaptation to the prison environment and the milder attitude of the jailers brought improvement in their lot.

The Barracks, the Prison Block and the Cell of Bahá'u'lláh

The citadel and barracks[3] to which the exiles had been consigned had been constructed at the northern edge of the city more than a half-century before, the barrack-square built as a khán by 'Alí Páshá, the squat square citadel strengthened by 'Abdu'lláh Páshá, his son. Both complexes were set upon the

massive foundations of the great chapter fortress of the Crusader Knights of the Hospital; both were built upon or added to earlier buildings of 'Umar, al-Jazzár and Sulaymán. Rough but functional, the new structures stood on the edge of the former inner moat and, since garrison needs were limited, they could be used as a prison, and were then termed by some 'the Turkish Bastille'. The isolation and pressures of imprisonment were usually compounded by mistreatment, by deliberate deprivations of food, and by such absence of any hygiene as would guarantee that enteric diseases, malaria and all the other host of epidemic and endemic sicknesses of that pestilential city would take their predictable toll of prisoners confined therein.

From the beginning Bahá'u'lláh and His family were confined to the upper floor of the north-west wing of the then almost empty barrack-square. The south-western room of that wing was assigned to the Blessed Beauty, a room which is now

North-west building of the 'Akká prison complex seen from the inner moat. The cell of Bahá'u'lláh is upper right. The upper floor was occupied by members of the Holy Family, the other exiles being confined on lower floors or elsewhere in the prison complex.

The Most Great Prison, place of the incarceration of Bahá'u'lláh

30

a Holy Place. Here He revealed the *Lawḥ-i-Ra'ís*, the *Lawḥ-i-Fu'ád*, and Tablets to Napoleon III and to Pope Pius IX.

In the eastern section of the upper floor, presently closed off by a wall, a staircase led upward to the roof, a skylight bringing some additional illumination. Áqá Mírzá Muḥammad-Qulí and his family lived on the lower floor. The others, including Mírzá Músá (Áqáy-i-Kalím) were held elsewhere in the barracks complex.[4]

...terior of the cell of ...ahá'u'lláh. The alcove ...ithout a window at the ...ft faces south; the alcove ...ith double windows at the ...ght faces the sea to the ...est. (Welsh, 1921)

Section of the north-west building assigned to the Holy Family; Bahá'u'lláh's cell is entered through the left doorway. Photograph taken prior to conversion of the cell block by the British authorities into a formal prison. (Welsh 1921)

The First Pilgrims

Towards the very end of the days in Adrianople, Bahá'u'lláh had quietly commissioned a devoted believer of <u>Sh</u>íráz, Mírzá 'Abdu'l-Aḥad, to go to the far-off city of 'Akká in Palestine, there to open a shop, meanwhile concealing his identity as a Bahá'í. Later the Prisoner and His companions arrived, to be incarcerated in the barracks. But, so tight was the confinement, so close the constant observation and so treacherous the Azalís, that for the first months in prison the Bahá'ís made no contact with Him. In the reported words of the Greatest Holy Leaf:

So great would his ['Abdu'l-Aḥad's] danger have been, had his connexion with the Bahá'ís been suspected, that the strictest caution was absolutely necessary.

Having heard a rumour that the Beloved Ones had been sent to 'Akká, a friend, Abu'l-Qásim <u>Kh</u>án, and his wife, made that long and dangerous journey from Persia in order to find out the truth. Arrived in 'Akká they met Mírzá 'Abdu'l-Aḥad. He, fearing lest his secret should be disclosed, hurriedly hid the pair behind stacks of boxes at the back of his shop.

The news of their arrival was, with much difficulty, conveyed to

View from Bahá'u'lláh's prison-cell area north-westward across the inner and outer moats

Bahá'u'lláh. He sent them back to Persia, after a stay of only three days, so grave was the risk. These friends accordingly left 'Akká. They had not even seen Bahá'u'lláh, but they were able to carry the news back to Persia that the Beloved Ones were really imprisoned in this desolate place.

The first Persian friends to telegraph to 'Akká were the 'King of the Martyred' [sic] and his brother, the 'Beloved of the Martyred'. (See p. 91) The help they succeeded in sending was much needed, as we were past the end of our resources. Little by little the news of our whereabouts filtered through to the other friends in Persia . . . (*The Chosen Highway*, p. 67)

Thus was the stage set for the first pilgrimages to this remote spot where the climactic chapter of Bahá'u'lláh's Ministry was opening. Soon came the first trickle of the faithful.

The few pilgrims who, despite the ban that had been so rigidly imposed, managed to reach the gates of the Prison – some of whom had journeyed the entire distance from Persia on foot – had to content themselves with a fleeting glimpse of the face of the Prisoner, as they stood, beyond the second moat, facing the window of His Prison. The very few who succeeded in penetrating into the city had, to their great distress, to retrace their steps without even beholding His countenance. The first among them, the self-denying Hájí Abu'l-Hasan-i-Ardikání, surnamed Amín-i-Iláhí (Trusted of God), to enter His presence was only able to do so in a public bath where it had been arranged that he should see Bahá'u'lláh without approaching Him or giving any sign of recognition. Another pilgrim, Ustád Ismá'íl-i-Káshí, arriving from Mosul, posted himself on the far side of the moat, and, gazing for hours, in rapt adoration, at the window of his Beloved, failed in the end, owing to the feebleness of his sight, to discern His face, and had to turn back to the cave which served as his dwelling-place on Mt. Carmel – an episode that moved to tears the Holy Family who had been anxiously watching from afar the frustration of his hopes. (*God Passes By*, pp. 187–8)

It seems likely that Hájí Amín-i-Iláhí arrived in 'Akká early in the year 1869, accompanied by Hájí Sháh-Muhammad. The bath built by al-Jazzár,[5] to which the prisoners were taken weekly on Fridays, comprised a chain of rooms, in the largest of which Hájí Amín and his friend were enabled surreptitiously to see Bahá'u'lláh. However, Hájí Amín was so overcome with emotion at being in the presence of Him Who was the Object of his veneration that he fainted, striking his head and bleeding from the wound. Bahá'u'lláh later penned Tablets to Hájí

Amín, honouring him as the first to visit 'This Wronged One', and saying in one of them:

Thou art the first one to attain the divine presence in His mighty, His Most Great Prison. Take heed lest what thou hast heard from the tongue of thy Lord, the Potent, the Powerful, be obliterated from thy heart. Make thou mention of Him all the time and call to mind the days when thou didst enter the most desolate of the cities until thou didst present thyself before the face of thy Lord, the Ruler of the Day of Judgement, and achieved that which is ordained for thee in His Preserved Tablet. (Translation from the Research Department, Bahá'í World Centre, Tablet AB 165/108)

The time had now come to find a messenger to convey

Principal room in the bath of al-Jazzár, to which Bahá'u'lláh and the other prisoners were brought each week, and where occurred the incident of Ḥájí Amín, the first Bahá'í pilgrim. The bath has now become the Municipal Museum of the City of 'Akká.

Bahá'u'lláh's weighty Message to the Sháh of Írán (the *Lawḥ-i-Sulṭán*); in a superscription He had made an appeal to 'God to send one of His servants, and to detach him from Contingent Being, and to adorn his heart with . . . strength and composure . . .' (See Browne, *A Traveller's Narrative*, vol. ii, p. 391) Some time early in 1869 arrived a hardy youth from Khurásán, the seventeen-year-old Áqá Buzurg, whose brave father Ḥájí 'Abdu'l-Majíd-i-Shálfurúsh had been one of the few survivors of the siege of Fort Shaykh Ṭabarsí. The youth was taken into the prison by arrangement of the Master. Twice he was summoned to the cell to see Bahá'u'lláh, an unusual privilege perhaps made possible by the leniency of the governor, who had been influenced by favourable reports of the prisoners from the Greek doctor Petro (Butros), and especially by the extraordinarily impressive character of 'Abdu'l-Bahá. Áqá Buzurg eagerly volunteered to be that servant of 'strength and composure'. He was accepted and the Tablet was delivered to him on Mount Carmel by Ḥájí Sháh-Muḥammad-i-Amín, the youth promptly setting forth for Persia. Long months later he delivered the Tablet to the Sháh and was martyred for his heroism. Bahá'u'lláh eulogized him in a number of Tablets, calling him Badí',[6] the Wonderful One, the 'Pride of the Martyrs'.

Another pilgrim, Nabíl-i-A'ẓam, arriving in the guise of a Bukhárán in October 1868,

. . . had to precipitately flee the city, where he had been recognized, had to satisfy himself with a brief glimpse of Bahá'u'lláh from across that same moat, and continued to roam the countryside around Nazareth, Haifa, Jerusalem and Hebron, until the gradual relaxation of restrictions enabled him to join the exiles. (*God Passes By*, p. 188)

Ultimately he spent eighty-one days in the prison with his Beloved, from 21 March to 9 June 1870.

The Sacrifice of the Purest Branch

The twenty-two-year-old Mírzá Mihdí, younger son of the Blessed Beauty and 'companion of His Exile' since Baghdád days, served as one of His amanuenses during the prison months. In June of the second year, Mírzá Mihdí climbed the narrow stairway to the roof, as was his wont, where he would walk and sometimes chant that heavenly poem of Bahá'u'lláh, the *Qaṣídiy-i-Varqá'íyyih* (the Ode of the Dove). Shoghi Effendi relates that he 'was pacing the roof of the barracks in the twilight, one evening, wrapped in his customary devotions, when he fell through the unguarded skylight on to a wooden crate, standing on the floor [ten metres] beneath, which pierced his ribs . . .' (The quotations in this section are taken from *God Passes By*, p. 188, and *The Bahá'í World*, vol. viii, pp. 247, 249, and 255–6) And Rúḥíyyih <u>Kh</u>ánum has given this touching description: 'The Purest Branch was terribly injured. He bled profusely from the mouth, and his thigh was so battered and bleeding that his garment could not be removed but was torn from him . . .' In the International Bahá'í Archives this 'pitiful relic which the Greatest Holy Leaf preserved for posterity . . . may be seen with the stains of his life's blood upon it.'

Mírzá Mihdí, Adrianople, 1868

As the hours slipped by, an Italian physician's treatment proved fruitless and there was no hospital in that grim city for the poor youth with his broken bones and pierced lungs. The Blessed Beauty Himself attended the dying youth, comforting His delicate and pious son 'to whose "meekness" the Supreme Pen had testified . . .' Bahá'u'lláh asked him 'if he desired to live, but he replied that his sole desire was that the gates of the prison should be opened so that the believers might visit their Lord', entreating his Father 'to accept him as a ransom for those of His loved ones who yearned for, but were unable to attain, His presence . . .'

Twenty-two hours after the fall, on the 23rd of Rabí'u'l-Avvál 1287 AH (23 June 1870), the loving and gentle Mírzá Mihdí passed to his Lord. His broken body was carried to a tent in the courtyard to be washed by <u>Sh</u>aykh Maḥmúd, while Bahá'u'lláh, Father and Prophet, sat beside his body and mourned for him:

At this very moment My son is being washed before My face, after Our having sacrificed him in the Most Great Prison. Thereat have the dwellers of the Abhá Tabernacle wept with a great weeping, [and] such as have suffered imprisonment with this Youth in the path of God, the Lord of the promised Day, lamented . . . This is the day whereon he that was created of the light of Bahá has suffered martyrdom, at a time when he lay imprisoned at the hands of his enemies.

Thereafter the mortal remains were 'borne forth, escorted by the fortress guards, and laid to rest, beyond the city walls, in a spot adjacent to the shrine of Nabí Ṣáliḥ . . .'

In honour and tribute to the Purest Branch the Blessed Beauty penned numerous verses. In one prayer He affirms: 'Glorified art Thou, O Lord, My God! Thou seest me in the hands of Mine enemies, and My son blood-stained before Thy face, O Thou in Whose hands is the kingdom of all names.' And Shoghi Effendi writes:

In a highly significant prayer, revealed by Bahá'u'lláh in memory of His son – a prayer that exalts his death to the rank of those great acts of atonement associated with Abraham's intended sacrifice of His son, with the crucifixion of Jesus Christ and the martyrdom of the Imám Ḥusayn – we read the following: 'I have, O my Lord, offered up that which Thou hast given Me, that Thy servants may be quickened, and all that dwell on earth be united.'

To the sorrowing Navváb Bahá'u'lláh gave assurance that 'she had no cause for grief for God had accepted this precious son as His Ransom to draw not only the believers nigh unto their Lord but to unify all the sons of men.'

Thereafter the harsh conditions in the prison were somewhat eased as the local officials grew to recognize the true character and greatness of the Prisoner, and as the power of the Master's personality and His innate wisdom were appreciated.

When Turkey reorganized its army in 1869 as one of its reforms of that period, 'Akká became the site of new military activities. The barracks were filled with soldiers quartered in the city. Bahá'u'lláh protested at the crowding and problems produced by the soldiers; hence, early in November 1870, the governor allowed the Great Prisoner and His followers to leave the barracks to live in the city under house confinement and surveillance. Mihdí's request and Bahá'u'lláh's promise were soon to be fulfilled, for pilgrims would attain His presence with ever greater ease and freedom.

Interior stairs in the eastern section of the north-west building leading from the upper floor to the roof; Mírzá Mihdí went up these stairs to his prayerful vigils.

8 Three Houses in the Western Quarter

THE BLESSED BEAUTY and the Holy Family were housed wherever room was available, while from the outset most of the other exiles were consigned to the Khán-i-'Avámíd, also known as the Inn of the Pillars or Khán al-'Umdán, there occupying many rooms, while Mírzá Músá at first occupied a house inside the square of the khán. Bahá'u'lláh Himself was moved to the house of Malik,[1] then after three months to that of Manṣúr Khavvám[2] which faced it across a narrow lane, both houses being located in the former Templar quarter near the Churches of St. George and St. Andrew in the Christian south-western part of the city. After a few months the family was transferred to a Muslim section, once the quarter of the merchants of Pisa during the Crusades, to live for another four months with the

The Khán-i-'Avámíd or Inn of the Pillars, northern section, showing the tower of Sultan 'Abdu'l-Ḥamíd, and the house in the courtyard probably once occupied by Áqáy-i-Kalím and his family.

The house of 'Údí Khammár in 'Akká, seen from Genoa (formerly 'Abbúd) Square. The windows at the upper left open into the room where the *Kitáb-i-Aqdas* was revealed. The middle-floor window opens into the *bírúní* of the house. The house of Tannús Farráh is at the right. A fountain, long removed, is seen at the right.

family of Rábi'ih, a charcoal-maker whose house was adjacent to the tiny Shrine of Shaykh Ghánim, a warrior of Saladin (Ṣaláḥ al-Dín).

At last, and surely with relief after the frequent moves, the Bahá'ís discovered an empty house: a wealthy Christian merchant had vacated his small town house to occupy a just-restored mansion, a veritable palace at the garden of Bahjí (Delight) located about two kilometres north-east of the city, just north of the great mansion of the Páshás Sulaymán and 'Abdu'lláh. Thus the Holy Family transferred to the house of 'Údí Khammár,[3] into the heart of the Christian community of 'Akká.

9 The House of 'Údí Khammár

'ÚDÍ KHAMMÁR had occupied the smaller, eastern part of a double house, his dwelling facing upon Genoa (then 'Abbúd) Square in

the former Genoese quarter, and looking towards the nearby Greek Orthodox Church of St. George, both dating back to the Crusades. The much larger house of Ilyás (Elias) 'Abbúd – often called <u>Kh</u>ájih (Esteemed) – stood to the west, facing the sea battlements and the Mediterranean beyond, a common wall dividing the two dwellings, with the ground floors of both houses used as business premises. The Holy Family moved into this small house, '. . . so insufficient to their needs that in one of its rooms no less than thirteen persons of both sexes had to accommodate themselves'. (*God Passes By*, p. 189) But it was a step towards freedom.

Crisis in the Community

At the time of the banishment from Adrianople two Azalís, Siyyid Muḥammad-i-Iṣfahání and Áqá Ján Big-i-Kaj-Kuláh, had been sent with the party of Bahá'ís. At this moment, in January 1872, when

Their strict confinement had hardly been mitigated, and the guards who had kept watch over them been dismissed, . . . an internal crisis, which had been brewing in the midst of the community, was brought to a sudden and catastrophic climax. Such had been the conduct of two of the exiles, who had been included in the party that accompanied Bahá'u'lláh to 'Akká, that He was eventually forced to expel them, an act of which Siyyid Muḥammad did not hesitate to take the fullest advantage. Reinforced by these recruits, he, together with his old associates, acting as spies, embarked on a campaign of abuse, calumny and intrigue, even more pernicious than that which had been launched by him in Constantinople, calculated to arouse an already prejudiced and suspicious populace to a new pitch of animosity and excitement. (*God Passes By*, p. 189)

The Bahá'ís, many of whom were resolute individuals, were intensely irritated by, among other mischief, the habit of the Azalís of watching, from the balcony of their lodging over the old 'Lion's Gate' on the main street leading to the land gate of the city, for the arrival of Persian pilgrims, and of reporting them to the authorities, thereby preventing their successful entry to the city. Moreover, they had long known that Siyyid Muḥammad[1] was an arch-intriguer bent upon evil, and was abetted in his spying and rumour-mongering by the rough and truculent Áqá Ján Big, an ex-Turkish artillery officer. As a

40

View down Saladin Street to the land gate, from the approximate position of the old Lion's Gate. At the right is the place of the old city jail.

consequence of the mounting friction between Bahá'ís and Azalís,

A fresh danger now clearly threatened the life of Bahá'u'lláh. Though He Himself had stringently forbidden His followers, on several occasions, both verbally and in writing, any retaliatory acts against their tormentors, and had even sent back to Beirut an irresponsible Arab convert, who had meditated avenging the wrongs suffered by his beloved Leader, seven of the companions clandestinely sought out and slew three of their persecutors, among whom were Siyyid Muḥammad and Áqá Ján. [On 22 January 1872. The third was Mírzá Riḍá-Qulíy-i-Tafríshí.]

The consternation that seized an already oppressed community was indescribable. Bahá'u'lláh's indignation knew no bounds. 'Were We', He thus voices His emotions, in a Tablet revealed shortly after this act had been committed, 'to make mention of what befell Us, the heavens would be rent asunder and the mountains would crumble.' 'My captivity', He wrote on another occasion, 'cannot harm Me. That which can harm Me is the conduct of those who love Me, who claim to be related to Me, and yet perpetrate what causeth My heart and My pen to groan.' And again: 'My captivity can bring on Me no shame. Nay, by My life, it conferreth on Me glory. That which can make Me ashamed is the conduct of such of My followers as profess to love Me, yet in fact follow the Evil One.'

He was dictating His Tablets to His amanuensis when the governor, at the head of his troops, with drawn swords, surrounded His house. The entire populace, as well as the military authorities, were in a state of great agitation. The shouts and clamour of the people

41

could be heard on all sides. Bahá'u'lláh was peremptorily summoned
to the Governorate, [and] interrogated . . .

'Is it proper', the Commandant of the city, turning to Bahá'u'lláh,
after He had arrived at the Governorate, boldly inquired, 'that some
of your followers should act in such a manner?' 'If one of your
soldiers', was the swift rejoinder, 'were to commit a reprehensible
act, would you be held responsible, and be punished in his place?'

. . . Bahá'u'lláh was . . . kept in custody the first night, with one of
His sons, in a chamber in the Khán-i-Shávirdí, [then] transferred for
the following two nights to better quarters in that neighbourhood

Eleventh-century Fatimid
Arab doorway into the
governorate of
Bahá'u'lláh's time, where
He was interrogated in
January 1872. The complex
is now used as a primary
school.

. . . 'Abdu'l-Bahá was thrown into prison and chained during the first night, after which He was permitted to join His Father . . .

In the afternoon of the third day Bahá'u'lláh was taken to the Governor's office.

. . . He was asked to state His name and that of the country from which He came. 'It is more manifest than the sun,' He answered. The same question was put to Him again, to which He gave the following reply: 'I deem it not proper to mention it. Refer to the farmán of the government which is in your possession.' Once again they, with marked deference, reiterated their request, whereupon Bahá'u'lláh spoke with majesty and power these words: 'My name is Bahá'u'lláh [Light of God], and My country is Núr [Light]. Be ye apprised of it.' Turning then, to the Muftí, He addressed him words of veiled rebuke, after which He spoke to the entire gathering, in such vehement and exalted language that none made bold to answer Him. Having quoted verses from the *Súriy-i-Mulúk*, He, afterwards, arose and left the gathering. The Governor, soon after, sent word that He was at liberty to return to His home, and apologized for what had occurred.

Seventy hours had elapsed from the time of His arrest.

A population, already ill-disposed towards the exiles, was, after such an incident, fired with uncontrollable animosity for all those who bore the name of the Faith which those exiles professed. The charges of impiety, atheism, terrorism and heresy were openly and without restraint flung into their faces. 'Abbúd, who lived next door to Bahá'u'lláh, reinforced the partition that separated his house from the dwelling of his now much-feared and suspected Neighbour. Even the children of the imprisoned exiles, whenever they ventured to show themselves in the streets during those days, would be pursued, vilified and pelted with stones.

The cup of Bahá'u'lláh's tribulations was now filled to overflowing. A situation, greatly humiliating, full of anxieties and even perilous, continued to face the exiles, until the time, set by an inscrutable Will, at which the tide of misery and abasement began to ebb, signalizing a transformation in the fortunes of the Faith even more conspicuous than the revolutionary change effected during the latter years of Bahá'u'lláh's sojourn in Baghdád. (Extracts, pp. 41–3, are from *God Passes By*, pp. 189–91)

The places where these events occurred, which marked the nadir of the Bahá'í fortunes in 'Akká, have been transformed with the passing of the decades. The court where Bahá'u'lláh was interrogated was then a part of the Governorate and is now a primary school situated between the Mosque of al-Jazzár and the Municipal Museum; its doorway is a fine Arab remnant of pre-Crusader times. The terrible prison where the seven accused Bahá'ís were held for seven years was immediately adjacent to the Khán-i-Shávirdí at its north-eastern corner, and next to what was then the inner gate of the city, the 'Lion's Gate' of Záhiru'l-'Umar. Sixteen innocent Bahá'ís were consigned to the khán in the very area where Bahá'u'lláh was detained for one night. The khán has gravely deteriorated and become a centre for ironworkers and ship repairmen; a road has been cut through its heart, passing the partially rehabilitated great Crusader tower, the Burju's-Sulṭán, at its south-eastern corner. It is not known precisely which room in the khán was occupied by the Blessed Beauty, but doubtless it was in the eastern wing next to the prison. The 'better quarters in that neighbourhood' where He was confined for two nights after His single night in the khán were above the Límán (prison).[2]

Aerial view of the governorate and its court room (1 and 2) in which Bahá'u'lláh suffered His interrogation in 1872. Near by are the barrack-square (3) and citadel (4), the Mosque of al-Jazzár (5), and its religious school (madrisih) (6). (1975)

The Marriage of 'Abdu'l-Bahá to Munírih Khánum

Soon after the transfer of the exiles from the barracks to houses in the city, there was renewed concern in the Holy Family for the twenty-seven-year-old 'Abbás, 'Abdu'l-Bahá, that it was timely for Him to marry.[3]

Not long thereafter, a girl from a distinguished family[4] of Iṣfahán, Fáṭimih Khánum, was called by the Blessed Beauty to the Holy Land. In Shavvál 1288 (December 1871–January 1872), she travelled with her brother Siyyid Yaḥyá and the courier Shaykh Salmán via Shíráz, where she was privileged to be often with the wife of the Báb during a two-weeks' stay; then by steamer to Jiddah and on to Mecca for pilgrimage, to conceal their real destination; next, to Alexandria; and finally, when it was prudent, they were directed by Bahá'u'lláh to come by boat to 'Akká. Upon arrival in 'Akká, they were met by 'Abdu'l-Aḥad, Áqáy-i-Kalím (Mírzá Músá) and Ilyás 'Abbúd, and the very next day she attained the presence of Bahá'u'lláh. Fáṭimih Khánum lived for some five months in the house of Áqáy-i-Kalím, during which time the Blessed Beauty often received her. He Himself bestowed upon her the name of Munírih (The Illumined One).

But there was a problem: no space for a bridal couple existed in the crowded quarters of the little house of 'Údí Khammár. The owner of the adjacent house, Ilyás 'Abbúd, had several times asked why the proposed marriage was being postponed; although no definite reason was given, he came to realize that the absence of a room for the couple was the obstacle. There-upon he offered to provide a room from his own house for the Master, furnished one which adjoined the little house on the top floor, opened a doorway into it through the dividing wall, and then presented the room to Bahá'u'lláh for the Master's use.

In late August or September 1872, it seems, the marriage night arrived, and Munírih donned a white robe and a white head-dress prepared for her by Ásíyih Khánum and Bahíyyih Khánum. At nine in the evening, in company with the Greatest Holy Leaf, she went into the presence of Bahá'u'lláh, Who said:

You are welcome! You are welcome! O thou My Blessed Leaf and Maid Servant! We have chosen thee and accepted thee to be the companion of the Greatest Branch and to serve Him. This is from

My Bounty, to which there is no equal; the treasures of the earth and heaven cannot be compared with it . . . Thou must be very thankful for thou hast attained to this most great favour and bestowal.

And He sent her away with the words: 'May you always be under the Protection of God.' (Munírih Khánum, *Episodes*, p. 30)

Going then to the bridal room she awaited the coming of her Beloved. At about ten o'clock 'Abdu'l-Bahá came, with the wife of Áqáy-i-Kalím, the wife and daughter of 'Abbúd, and the mother of Muḥammad-'Alí, who brought the special Tablets revealed by Bahá'u'lláh for such occasions. When asked to do so, Munírih Khánum then chanted, in a clear and resonant voice, the Tablet which begins with the joyous declaration:

> Verily, the doors of Paradise are opened and the divine Youth hath appeared! (ibid.)

Later, the wife of 'Abbúd recalled the sweetness of that chanting still ringing in her ears, saying: 'Never before in this world have I heard a bride chanting at her own wedding.' (ibid.)[5]

Revelation of the Book of Laws

The Prophet's last months of 1872 and into early 1873 were overwhelmingly significant, for it was then that the 'brightest emanation of the Mind of Bahá'u'lláh', 'The Mother Book of His Dispensation', the *Kitáb-i-Aqdas*, was elaborated.

Revealed soon after Bahá'u'lláh had been transferred to the house of Údí Khammár (*circa* 1873), at a time when He was still encompassed by the tribulations that had afflicted Him, through the acts committed by His enemies and the professed adherents of His Faith, this Book, this treasury enshrining the priceless gems of His Revelation, stands out, by virtue of the principles it inculcates, the administrative institutions it ordains and the function with which it invests the appointed Successor of its Author, unique and incomparable among the world's sacred Scriptures. (*God Passes By*, p. 213)

The laws and ordinances that constitute the major theme of this Book,[6] Bahá'u'lláh, moreover, has specifically characterized as 'the breath of life unto all created things', as 'the mightiest stronghold', as the 'fruits' of His 'Tree', as 'the highest means for the maintenance of order in the world and the security of its peoples', as 'the lamps of

The room of Bahá'u'lláh in the House of 'Údí Khammár, where He revealed His Book of Laws, the *Kitáb-i-Aqdas*. The two windows look eastward into Genoa Square. 'Abdu'l-Bahá later occupied this room, installing the wooden panelling now seen.

46

His wisdom and loving-providence', as 'the sweet smelling savour of His garment', as the 'keys' of His 'mercy' to His creatures. 'This Book', He Himself testifies, 'is a heaven which We have adorned with the stars of Our commandments and prohibitions ' . . . 'Say, O men! Take hold of it with the hand of resignation . . . By My life! It hath been sent down in a manner that amazeth the minds of men. Verily, it is My weightiest testimony unto all people, and the proof of the All-Merciful unto all who are in heaven and all who are on earth.' And again: 'Blessed the palate that savoureth its sweetness, and the perceiving eye that recognizeth that which is treasured therein, and the understanding heart that comprehendeth its allusions and mysteries. By God! Such is the majesty of what hath been revealed therein, and so tremendous the revelation of its veiled allusions that the loins of utterance shake when attempting their description.' And finally: 'In such a manner hath the *Kitáb-i-Aqdas* been revealed that it attracteth and embraceth all the divinely appointed Dispensations . . . So vast is its range that it hath encompassed all men ere their recognition of it. Erelong will its sovereign power, its pervasive influence and the greatness of its might be manifested on earth.' (ibid. pp. 215–16)

When the text of the *Kitáb-i-Aqdas* was made available, the questions it called forth from Jináb-i-Zaynu'l-Muqarrabín with Bahá'u'lláh's replies became that important appendix to the *Aqdas* which is known simply as *Questions and Answers*.

Concerning the implementation of the laws themselves Bahá'u'lláh

wrote in one of His Tablets: 'Indeed the laws of God are like unto the ocean and the children of men as fish, did they but know it. However, in observing them one must exercise tact and wisdom . . . Since most people are feeble and far-removed from the purpose of God, therefore one must observe tact and prudence under all conditions, so that nothing might happen that could cause disturbance and dissension or raise clamour among the heedless. Verily, His bounty hath surpassed the whole universe and His bestowals encompassed all that dwell on earth. One must guide mankind to the ocean of true understanding in a spirit of love and tolerance. The *Kitáb-i-Aqdas* itself beareth eloquent testimony to the loving providence of God.' (*Synopsis and Codification*, pp. 4–5)

In this Most Holy Book Bahá'u'lláh declares: 'By My life, if you knew what We have desired for you in revealing Our holy laws, you would offer up your souls for this sacred, mighty and lofty Cause.' 'This Book is none other than the ancient Lamp of God for the whole world and His undeviating Path amongst men. Say, it is verily the Dayspring of divine knowledge, did ye but know it, and the Dawning-place of the commandments of God, could ye but comprehend it.' 'Say, this is the spirit of the Scriptures breathed into the Pen of Glory, causing all creation to be dumbfounded, except those who are stirred by the vitalizing fragrance of My tender mercy and the sweet savours of My bounty which pervade all created things.' (ibid. p. 7)

Imprisonment Ameliorated

The gradual recognition by all elements of the population of Bahá'u'lláh's complete innocence; the slow penetration of the true spirit of His teachings through the hard crust of their indifference and bigotry; the substitution of the sagacious and humane governor, Aḥmad Big Tawfíq, for one whose mind had been hopelessly poisoned against the Faith and its followers; the unremitting labours of 'Abdu'l-Bahá, now in the full flower of His manhood, Who, through His contacts with the rank and file of the population, was increasingly demonstrating His capacity to act as the shield of His Father; the providential dismissal of the officials who had been instrumental in prolonging the confinement of the innocent companions – all paved the way for the reaction that was now setting in . . . (*God Passes By*, p. 191)

The ground-swell of favourable reaction had occurred in large part because of the Master's constant loving endeavours in promoting understanding and good will. At some time during the early days when 'Abdu'l-Bahá was given greater freedom to go about in the city, He began, with permission of Bahá'u'lláh, to attend the principal mosque, that of al-Jazzár. This was the same mosque where had been read the firman of Sultan 'Abdu'l-'Azíz sentencing the Bahá'ís to banishment and imprisonment, and forbidding the admission of other Bahá'ís into the city. The Master now came into frequent contact with the religious and secular notables of 'Akká through His frequent visits to the mosque, with its associated institutions of madrisih (school), Sharí'ah court and civil offices. His discourses with all and sundry revealed to them His sagacity, depth of knowledge and grasp of human realities which soon made Him the acquaintance and often the counsellor of various Muslim personalities. There too He regularly gave alms to the poor.

An early element in the improved relationships with Muslim and Christian leaders in 'Akká was the friendship during prison days of the future Muftí of 'Akká, Shaykh Maḥmúd 'Arrábí,[7] 'a man notorious for his bigotry' who, upon his later becoming a Bahá'í, 'fired by his newborn enthusiasm, made a compilation of the Muhammadan traditions related to 'Akká', a study which he humbly presented to Bahá'u'lláh. (Quotations from *God Passes By*, p. 192. A Muftí is responsible for giving judgements or opinions on points of religious jurisprudence.)

A later Muftí, Shaykh 'Alíy-i-Mírí, whose house stood at the

The Mosque of al-Jazzár in 1840, at the time of the recapture of 'Akká from the Egyptians by the British and Turks

southern edge of the former Governorate of 'Abdu'lláh Páshá and was connected with its wall by a heavy archway with rooms above it, became a friend and admirer of Bahá'u'lláh and was that persuasive notable who was to be the final influence in His agreeing to leave the prison city for Mazra'ih in 1877 (see p. 87).

Doubtless the friendship and admiration of Colonel Aḥmad Jarráḥ,[8] prison commandant, who accepted the Faith along with his brothers Khálid and Amín[9] during Bahá'u'lláh's days in the House of 'Abbúd, was a further factor in the altered attitude of the people.

With the favour and even the homage of such religious and lay dignitaries as these, the Master was enabled to use a room at the edge of the court of the mosque, in its madrisih, the religious school. To this room, with its quiet and in the spiritual presence of the house of worship, He would retire at intervals for prayer and meditation as well as for brief freedom from the pressures of ever-more-demanding Bahá'í services.

The Mosque of al-Jazzár, its minaret restored in recent years after earthquake damage. In the foreground are the arches of the White Súq, built by Ẓáhiru'l-'Umar and restored by Sulaymán Páshá. The dome at the right marks the site of the Muslim Sharí'ah Court of 'Akká district. (1981)

10 The House of 'Abbúd

IN THE CLIMATE of improving relations within the prison city, and with the outflow of Revelation in full tide, the Holy Family received a new bounty. 'Abbúd, the now friendly neighbour, was ill, wished to leave the city and to rent his house to Bahá'u'lláh. With alacrity the house was taken, and now there was abundant space for the Holy Family and those who served it. A doorway was broken through the common wall, on the topmost floor, fusing the two upper courts, and on the ground floor a doorway was also cut for access between the houses. Bahá'u'lláh moved forthwith to the spacious, many-windowed, high-ceilinged upper room in the south-western corner, a light and airy room which opened into a passageway leading to a beautiful gallery overlooking the sea. Next door was the room of His wife, the beloved Navváb, while to 'Abdu'l-Bahá was given the room where the *Kitáb-i-Aqdas* had been revealed. The Master's growing family thereafter lived in what was called 'the small house' of 'Údí Khammár; and for His work of counsel and assistance to others a *bírúní* was rented, a room across Genoa Square.[1]

Even in the double house, which thereafter was to be known only as the House of 'Abbúd, there was not enough private accommodation, for the families of the exiles were expanding.[2] But the far more commodious quarters made possible a new level of activity, for there was room for work, for reception of the increasing numbers of pilgrims, and for a better life for the friends who circled about the Blessed Beauty. In this house continued that effusion of the 'subsidiary ordinances designed to supplement the provisions of His Most Holy Book',[3] an outpouring of Revelation which was to be sustained to the end of Bahá'u'lláh's life. And from this house Bahá'u'lláh was able to visit the Khán-i-'Avámíd, and on occasion other places in the city.

During the governorship of Aḥmad Big Tawfíq there came a

recognition of the power of Bahá'u'lláh. Indeed,

Such was the devotion gradually kindled in the heart of that governor, through his association with 'Abdu'l-Bahá, and later through his perusal of the literature of the Faith, which mischief-makers, in the hope of angering him, had submitted for his consideration, that he invariably refused to enter His presence without first removing his shoes, as a token of his respect for Him. It was even bruited about that his favoured counsellors were those very exiles who were the followers of the Prisoner in his custody. His own son he was wont to send to 'Abdu'l-Bahá for instruction and enlightenment. It was on the occasion of a long-sought audience with Bahá'u'lláh that, in response to a request for permission to render Him some service, the suggestion was made to him to restore the aqueduct which for thirty years had been allowed to fall into disuse – a suggestion which he immediately arose to carry out.[4] To the inflow of pilgrims, among whom were numbered the devout and venerable Mullá Ṣádiq-i-Khurásání and the father of Badí', both survivors of the struggle of Ṭabarsí, he offered scarcely any opposition, though the text of the imperial farmán forbade their admission into the city. Muṣṭafá Ḍíyá Páshá, who became governor a few years later, had even gone so far as to intimate that his Prisoner was free to pass through its gates whenever He pleased, a suggestion which Bahá'u'lláh declined . . . Nor were the occasionally unsympathetic governors, despatched to that city, able, despite the arbitrary power they wielded, to check the forces which were carrying the Author of the Faith towards His

52

virtual emancipation and the ultimate accomplishment of His purpose . . .

Though Bahá'u'lláh Himself practically never granted personal interviews, as He had been used to do in Baghdád, yet such was the influence He now wielded that the inhabitants openly asserted that the noticeable improvement in the climate and water of their city was directly attributable to His continued presence in their midst. The very designations by which they chose to refer to Him, such as the 'august leader', and 'his highness' bespoke the reverence with which He inspired them. On one occasion, a European general who, together with the governor, was granted an audience by Him, was so impressed that he 'remained kneeling on the ground near the door'. (*God Passes By*, pp. 191–2)

'Abdu'l-Bahá has written:

The rulers of Palestine envied His influence and power. Governors and mutiṣarrifs, generals and local officials, would humbly request the honour of attaining His presence – a request to which He seldom acceded. (ibid. p. 193)

Bahá'u'lláh Himself has written of the first nine years of His banishment:

'Know thou, that upon Our arrival at this Spot, We chose to designate it as the "Most Great Prison". Though previously subjected in another land [Ṭihrán] to chains and fetters, We yet refused to call it by that name. Say: Ponder thereon, O ye endued with understanding!' (ibid. p. 185)

'Abdu'l-Bahá, characterizing Bahá'u'lláh's years in 'Akká, has stated:

'This illustrious Being uplifted His Cause in the Most Great Prison. From this Prison His light was shed abroad; His fame conquered the world, and the proclamation of His glory reached the East and the West.' 'His light at first had been a star; now it became a mighty sun.' 'Until our time, no such thing has ever occurred.' (ibid. p. 196)

The House of 'Abbúd from present-day Haganah Street, with its gallery surrounding the room of Bahá'u'lláh on the upper floor; the doorway into the House from the alley leading into Genoa Square is also seen.

Little wonder that, in view of so remarkable a reversal in the circumstances attending the twenty-four years of His banishment to 'Akká, Bahá'u'lláh Himself should have penned these weighty words: 'The Almighty . . . hath transformed this Prison-House into the Most Exalted Paradise, the Heaven of Heavens.' (ibid.)

There soon came a time when the Muftí and other Muslim

friends in 'Akká repeatedly asserted that Bahá'u'lláh's restriction to the prison city was ended. In order to test the truth of these statements, towards the end of spring in 1877 'Abdu'l-Bahá obtained the permission of its Christian owner Jirjis (Georges) al-Jamál to use the grove of some eighteen pine trees on the property immediately adjacent to 'Údí Khammár's mansion, and He invited the notables of 'Akká to a banquet under the trees. When they accepted the hospitality of the once-vilified exiles from Persia, the Master knew clearly that

The drastic farmán of Sulṭán 'Abdu'l-'Azíz, though officially unrepealed, had by now become a dead letter. Though Bahá'u'lláh was still nominally a prisoner, 'the doors of majesty and true sovereignty were', in the words of 'Abdu'l-Bahá, 'flung wide open'. (ibid. p. 193)

The pines of Bahjí on the land of the Jamál brothers, site of the dinner which signalled the opening of the gates of 'Akká and the freeing of the Great Prisoner. In the background are the Shrine and Mansion of Bahjí. (Getsinger, *c.* 1900)

Now the Most Great Prison was no longer a place of confinement. With the opening of its gates to Bahá'u'lláh a great chapter in religious history had ended.

54

11 'Abdu'l-Bahá in 'Akká: 1877–1892

AFTER THE DEPARTURE of Bahá'u'lláh for Mazra'ih (see p. 88), 'Abdu'l-Bahá remained with His expanding family in the House of 'Abbúd, in that half originally occupied by 'Údí Khammár. There nine children were born to Munírih Khánum, two boys and seven girls. One boy, Mihdí, and two girls died in infancy. One daughter passed away at fifteen, but four daughters grew to maturity despite the arduous years in the dangerous, disease-ridden town: they were Díyá'íyyih, Túbá, Rúhá and Munavvar.

Little Husayn, who became the delight of his Grandfather and who stayed at Bahjí for long intervals, died at the age of four in 1888. Munírih Khánum recalled that 'When my darling little son Husayn passed away, Bahá'u'lláh wrote the following: "The knowledge of the reason why your sweet baby has been called back is in the mind of God, and will be manifested in His own good time. To the prophets of God the present and the future are as one." ' Husayn was an eager, sprightly child, delighting in new experiences, new small adventures, often entreating his beloved Grandfather to take him on little walks to see new sights. Thus, upon his much-grieved passing Bahá'u'lláh Himself penned an epitaph for the little boy's tombstone, saying:

He is the Eternal!

Husayn, son of 'Ayn[1]
  Wealth and children are the adornment of this present life; but good works, which are lasting, are better in the sight of thy Lord as to recompense and better as to hope.[2]
  This son was an adornment of the most Exalted Paradise. Through God's Grace and Bounty . . . we see him now engaged in sightseeing[3] in the heavenly realms.

  1305 AH [1888] (Translation from the Research Department, Bahá'í World Centre)

During the years from 1877 to 1892 the Master became ever more the indefatigable counsellor and manager of mundane affairs for His Father and the Bahá'í community, vigilant of the welfare of Bahá'ís and others even as His roles of direct and indirect service to the Cause itself were expanding. Among His services to the needy of 'Akká was His payment of a doctor Nicolá to provide medical care. He wrote for the friends in Persia that extraordinary book known in the West by the title: *The Secret of Divine Civilization*,[4] characterized by Shoghi Effendi as His 'outstanding contribution to the future reorganization of the world'. (Shoghi Effendi, *The World Order of Bahá'u'lláh*, p. 37) Later He penned *A Traveller's Narrative*, described as 'written to illustrate The Episode of the Báb', that brief history of the Faith's beginnings which was given to the English orientalist Edward G. Browne on the occasion of his visit to Bahá'u'lláh in the spring of 1890. Then, as throughout His lifetime, the Master carried on an immense correspondence, using His 'tired hours' for this labour of love on behalf of the believers of the Orient and, later, of the Bahá'í world.[5]

The inflow of pilgrims continued apace, and 'Abdu'l-Bahá undertook many aspects of their care and assistance, overseeing their housing and nourishment, and often escorting them Himself to the presence of the Blessed Beauty. The House of 'Abbúd itself was a place of pilgrimage, with the room of Bahá'u'lláh preserved inviolate.

Most memorable of all moments of those busy and productive years were the visits of the Manifestation Himself, Who returned a number of times during the latter years of His life to this House where the *Kitáb-i-Aqdas* and many Tablets had been revealed.

During this period of waxing favour towards Bahá'u'lláh and the Master among the people and officials in and about 'Akká, there were a number of important events, as described by the Guardian:

'Abdu'l-Bahá as a young man in Adrianople in 1868

'Abdu'l-Bahá's visit to Beirut, at the invitation of Midḥat Páshá, a former Grand Vizir of Turkey, occurring about this time [1879]; His association with the civil and ecclesiastical leaders of that city; His several interviews with the well-known Shaykh Muḥammad 'Abdu served to enhance immensely the growing prestige of the community and spread abroad the fame of its most distinguished member. The splendid welcome accorded him by the learned and highly esteemed Shaykh Yúsuf, the Muftí of Nazareth, who acted as host to the válís of Beirut, and who had despatched all the notables of the community several miles on the road to meet Him as He approached the town, accompanied by His brother and the Muftí of 'Akká, as well as the magnificent reception given by 'Abdu'l-Bahá to that same Shaykh Yúsuf when the latter visited Him in 'Akká, were such as to arouse the envy of those who, only a few years before, had treated Him and His fellow-exiles with feelings compounded of condescension and scorn. (*God Passes By*, p. 193)

During this period, also, 'Properties bordering on the Lake [the Sea of Galilee] associated with the ministry of Jesus Christ, were, moreover, purchased at Bahá'u'lláh's bidding . . .' (ibid. p. 194) The now-liberated exiles were free to settle in the places where they wished or were directed by Bahá'u'lláh. Thus, departing from 'Akká, the loyal half-brother, Mírzá Muhammad-Qulí, and his family settled on lands purchased in the name of Bahá'u'lláh Himself in the Jordan valley, an extensive acreage on the eastern shore of the Sea of Galilee (Lake Kinneret) in the area then called Nuqayb, now Ein Gev, at the foot of the Golan escarpment, just beneath the ruins of the ancient Hellenic city of Hippos, or Susita. Mírzá Muhammad-Qulí's daughters and their families later settled at the south-eastern edge of the lake, near the hamlet of Samras. Still other families became farmers and herdsmen in the village of 'Adasíyyih on the hill-slopes just across the Yarmuk River near its Jordan confluence.

Munírih Khánum, wife of 'Abdu'l-Bahá

In the House of 'Abbúd, during the residence of Bahá'u'lláh, His beloved wife Navváb had been given the room next to His own, and in this very room she passed to the Abhá Kingdom in 1886, to be most sorrowfully interred in the Bahá'í section of the Muslim cemetery. No longer would the gentle person of Bahá'u'lláh's 'consort in all the worlds of God' be present to support her beloved Son and daughter or her adored Husband, Whom she had followed with utter devotion and loyalty through fifty-one years of marriage, of prosperity and destitution, of exile after exile until the final fulfilment of His Revelation in that very House.

When, in 1887 in 'Akká, the steadfast Mírzá Músá, Áqáy-i-Kalím, who had espoused the Bábí Cause almost in the same hour as his Brother, passed to the Abhá Kingdom, another great pillar of the Faith was removed. With his passing a benign and unwavering loyalty was removed from Bahá'u'lláh's family and companions.

The pilgrims from Persia continued to arrive and were housed in 'Akká under the Master's wing, many at the Khán-i-'Avámíd. Some, like the ardent youth Ṭarázu'lláh Samandarí, were destined for great service to the Cause. Others gained confirmation and strength for their hard lives of teaching under persecution in Persia. And guests of all kinds who wished audience with Bahá'u'lláh were often the special charge of the Master, as with the orientalist Edward G. Browne.

Then, with the passing of Bahá'u'lláh in 1892, when His Will and Testament named 'Abdu'l-Bahá as His Successor, there began the Ministry of Him Who became the Centre of His Covenant, the Exemplar of His Faith and the Interpreter of His Revelation.

Mírzá Músá,
Áqáy-i-Kalím, loyal
brother of Bahá'u'lláh

12 The House of 'Abdu'lláh Páshá

BEFORE HE BEGAN His Ministry in 1892, 'Abdu'l-Bahá had been singularly prepared for His tasks of leadership and of interpretation of the Word of Bahá'u'lláh. Two years earlier Edward Granville Browne had encountered the Master, thereafter penning a memorable description of Him:

Seldom have I seen one whose appearance impressed me more. A tall, strongly-built man holding himself straight as an arrow, with white turban and raiment, long black locks reaching almost to the shoulder, broad powerful forehead, indicating a strong intellect combined with an unswerving will, eyes keen as a hawk's, and strongly marked but pleasing features – such was my first impression of 'Abbás Efendi . . . Subsequent conversation with him served only to heighten the respect with which his appearance had from the first inspired me. One more eloquent of speech, more ready of argument, more apt of illustration, more intimately acquainted with the sacred books of the Jews, the Christians, and the Muhammadans, could, I should think, scarcely be found even amongst the eloquent, ready, and subtle race to which he belongs. These qualities, combined with a bearing at once majestic and genial, made me cease to wonder at the influence and esteem which he enjoyed even beyond the circle of his father's followers. About the greatness of this man and his power no one who had seen him could entertain a doubt. (Browne, *A Traveller's Narrative*, vol. ii, xxxvi)

Yet that summer of 1892 was a time of tragedy for the loving, creative Master, Who recognized so well the evil vapours of jealousy and of hunger for power and prestige in that half-brother whom He had so encouraged and supported. In sorrow and almost despair at the perfidy of members of His own family, and of so many of those who might confidently have been expected to give implicit obedience to the Will of Bahá'u'lláh, He betook Himself to Haifa and Mount Carmel and for a month isolated Himself in a small apartment of the stone building just west of the mouth of the lower Cave of Elijah. Returning to the House of 'Abbúd, He occupied the room across the hallway from the one hallowed by Bahá'u'lláh, and here He could contemplate the serene vastness of the sea and gain some respite from the ceaseless machinations of those now in open rebellion against the Master's succession to authority in the Faith.

The unwavering support of the Greatest Holy Leaf, and that of His wife and family, were the pillars of 'Abdu'l-Bahá's strength during those trying days. The Hands of the Cause too were defenders of the Faith, indefatigable in disproving the many falsities spread by the Covenant-breakers in Persia as in the Holy Land. At the World's Parliament of Religion in Chicago in 1893 the paper of the Reverend Henry H. Jessup had first mentioned the name of Bahá'u'lláh and quoted His words to a large gathering in the West. Before long, reports of the expansion of the Faith to the West brought joy to the Master: in Paris and London, as already in Chicago and New York, adherents were being found. And as the years passed, it became evident that most of the friends sensibly rejected the claims and allegations of Muḥammad-'Alí, and the threat of a serious schism steadily ebbed away.

During these days of tribulation the daughters of 'Abdu'l-Bahá were maturing. Thus, before he had returned to Persia after pilgrimage in 1892, Mírzá Hádí Afnán and his family had sought his marriage to Ḍíyá'íyyih Khánum, eldest daughter of the Master. The request was timely, and in 1896 the young

Afnán came from S͟híráz to wed her in a simple ceremony which brought joy to the hearts of the Holy Family.

The House of 'Abdu'lláh Pás͟há

In the course of the fourth year after Bahá'u'lláh's passing it became apparent that the portion of the House of 'Abbúd available for occupation was inadequate for His enlarged family. With characteristic vigour 'Abdu'l-Bahá took action and towards the end of the year (c. October) 1896 arranged to rent the main building of the former Governorate of 'Abdu'lláh Pás͟há[1] in the Mujádalih Quarter in the north-western corner of the city. He established it as His official residence, and as a home also for His daughters, their husbands and families.

Thus it came about that in March 1897, in an upper room of the south wing, a child was born who was ordained to hold the destiny of the Faith in his hands for thirty-six years and to become its 'beloved Guardian', the child named Shoghi by his Grandfather, who grew up under His loving and solicitous care and whose family name was to be Rabbani, 'divine', a name

given by that same knowing Grandparent.

The Guardian's childhood and upbringing in that house are warmly described by Amatu'l-Bahá Rúḥíyyih Khánum in *The Priceless Pearl*:

It may sound disrespectful to say the Guardian was a mischievous child, but he himself told me he was the acknowledged ringleader of all the other children. Bubbling with high spirits, enthusiasm and daring, full of laughter and wit, the small boy led the way in many pranks; whenever something was afoot, behind it would be found Shoghi Effendi! This boundless energy was often a source of anxiety as he would rush madly up and down the long flight of high steps to the upper storey of the house, to the consternation of the pilgrims below, waiting to meet the Master. His exuberance was irrepressible and was in the child the same force that was to make the man such an untiring and unflinching commander-in-chief of the forces of Bahá'u'lláh, leading them to victory after victory, indeed, to the spiritual conquest of the entire globe. We have a very reliable witness to this characteristic of the Guardian, 'Abdu'l-Bahá Himself, Who wrote on a used envelope a short sentence to please His little grand-son: 'Shoghi Effendi is a wise man – but he runs about very much!'. . .

In those days of Shoghi Effendi's childhood it was the custom to rise about dawn and spend the first hour of the day in the Master's room, where prayers were said and the family all had breakfast with Him. The children sat on the floor, their legs folded under them, their arms folded across their breasts, in great respect; when asked they would chant for 'Abdu'l-Bahá; there was no shouting or unseemly conduct. Breakfast consisted of tea, brewed on the bubbling Russian brass samovar and served in little crystal glasses, very hot and very sweet, pure wheat bread and goats' milk cheese. (pp. 7–8)

It was to this house that the historic first group of pilgrims from the West came to see the Master in the winter of 1898–9. That first group, arriving on 10 December 1898, was led by Mrs Phoebe Hearst and included Mrs Lua Getsinger, Miss May Bolles, Mrs Thornburgh-Cropper, and Mr Robert Turner. Many more from both East and West sought His presence in that blessed spot, and some have left memorable descriptions of their experiences with 'Abdu'l-Bahá and His household. Ella Goodall Cooper, a member of that first pilgrimage group, and one of the very earliest American believers, records the following:

One day . . . I had joined the ladies of the Family in the room of the

erial photograph showing
e complex, outlined in
hite, called the House of
bdu'lláh Páshá, at the
orth-western corner of the
alled city. The house of
e governor is at the upper
ght, with a row of
orkshops adjacent. Of the
ain building in the centre,
e southern and western
ings were used by the
Master and His family. In
ter years the northern
ing was used by members
f His family and
ousehold, and for housing
ilgrims. (1975)

Southern face of the House of 'Abdu'lláh Páshá, showing archway leading to the main door. On the upper floor (right) the two windows are of the room of the Greatest Holy Leaf, where the Holy Dust of the Báb was concealed for ten years.

Greatest Holy Leaf for early morning tea, the beloved Master was sitting in His favourite corner of the divan where, through the window on His right, He could look over the ramparts and see the blue Mediterranean beyond. He was busy writing Tablets, and the quiet peace of the room was broken only by the bubble of the samovar, where one of the young maidservants, sitting on the floor before it, was brewing tea. (*The Bahá'í World*, vol. xvi, p. 104)

Thornton Chase, the first American believer, records in his memoir *In Galilee*:

We did not know we had reached our destination until we saw a Persian gentleman, and then another and another, step out at the entrance and smile at us. We alighted and they conducted us through the arched, red-brick entrance to an open court, across it to a long flight of stone steps, broken and ancient, leading to the highest storey and into a small walled court open to the sky, where was the upper chamber assigned to us, which adjoined the room of 'Abdu'l-Bahá. The buildings are all of stone, whitewashed and plastered, and it bears the aspect of a prison.

Our windows looked out over the garden and tent of 'Abdu'l-

Bahá on the sea side of the house. That garden is bounded on one side by the house of the Governor, which overlooks it, and on another by the inner wall of fortification. A few feet beyond that is the outer wall upon the sea, and between these two are the guns and soldiers constantly on guard. A sentry house stands at one corner of the wall and garden, from which the sentry can see the grounds and the tent where 'Abdu'l-Bahá meets transient visitors and the officials who often call on him. Thus all his acts outside of the house itself are visible to the Governor from his windows and to the men on guard. Perhaps that is one reason why the officials so often become his friends. No one, with humanity, justice, or mercy in his heart, could watch 'Abdu'l-Bahá long without admiring and loving him for the beautiful qualities constantly displayed. (ibid. pp. 104–5)

Mary Hanford Ford published an account of her pilgrimage

Inner court of the House of 'Abdu'lláh Páshá, showing the stairs to the western and southern wings. Seen are the small garden which once graced the courtyard, one of the two palm-trees, the upper window (centre) opening into the Master's study, the lower two (right) into the bath area. (1921)

63

to this house in *Star of the West*, vol. xxiv, p. 105:

The little room in which I stayed and in which the significant conversations with 'Abdu'l-Bahá took place, was of the simplest description. The floor was covered with matting, the narrow iron bed and the iron wash stand with larger and smaller holes for bowl and pitcher were of that vermin-proof description with which I had become familiar. Everything was scrupulously clean, and there was an abundant supply of sparkling water for bathing and drinking. A wide window looked over the huge town wall upon the blue Mediterranean and before this stretched a divan upon which 'Abdu'l-Bahá sat when He came to see me. (ibid. p. 106)

T. K. Cheyne in his book *The Reconciliation of Races and Religions* reports a visitor's description of the way of life of 'Abdu'l-Bahá during His busy days in that house:

His general order for the day is prayers and tea at sunrise, and dictating letters or 'tablets', receiving visitors, and giving alms to the poor until dinner in the middle of the day. After this meal he takes a

The stairway from the inner court of the House of 'Abdu'lláh Páshá rising to the southern and western wings (Thornton Chase, 1907)

The room of 'Abdu'l-Bahá here He conversed with ilgrims in the House of Abdu'lláh Páshá (Chase,)07)

half-hour's siesta, spends the afternoon in making visits to the sick and others whom he has occasion to see about the city, and the evening in talking to the believers or in expounding, to any who wish to hear him, the Kuran, on which, even among Muslims, he is reputed to be one of the highest authorities, learned men of that faith frequently coming from great distances to consult him with regard to its interpretation.

He then returns to his house and works until about one o'clock over his correspondence. This is enormous, and would more than occupy his entire time, did he read and reply to all his letters personally. As he finds it impossible to do this, but is nevertheless determined that they shall all receive careful and impartial attention, he has recourse to the assistance of his daughter Rúḥá, upon whose intelligence and conscientious devotion to the work he can rely. During the day she reads and makes digests of letters received, which she submits to him at night.

The stairway from the inner court rising to the northern complex of rooms. The courtyard garden and two palm-trees are seen. (Chase, 1907)

And Mr. Cheyne, himself, comments:

In his charities he is absolutely impartial; his love is like the divine love – it knows no bounds of nation or creed. Most of those who benefit by his presence are of course Muslims; many true stories are current among his family and intimate friends respecting them. Thus, there is the story of the Afghan who for twenty-four years received the bounty of the good Master, and greeted him with abusive speeches. In the twenty-fifth year, however, his obstinacy broke. (pp. 160–61)

In this house, fifty lunar years after the Báb's martyrdom, on 31 January 1899, the casket containing His sacred and precious Remains was received by 'Abdu'l-Bahá, after it had been brought in concealment from Persia. The Master hid the blessed Dust in the room of the Greatest Holy Leaf until it was possible to inter it with all honours in its permanent resting-place in the bosom of Carmel.

It was in this house that His celebrated table talks were given and recorded by Laura Clifford Barney in the course of her pilgrimages from 1904 to 1906. They were compiled and published later under the title *Some Answered Questions.*

The south-east corner of the outer court of the House of 'Abdu'lláh Páshá, showing the house of the governor (centre), the Mujádalih Mosque (left), workshops (right). Pilgrims entered the compound from the street through a gate under the governor's house, emerging into the court from the archway seen at ground level (centre).

Renewal of Incarceration of 'Abdu'l-Bahá: 1901–1908

For 'Abdu'l-Bahá the twentieth century began with important successes in the expansion of the Faith, now emerging under His guidance to demonstrate its true destiny as the religion of all mankind. Yet the breakers of the Covenant were simmering a new stew. The increased machinations of Mírzá Muḥammad-'Alí were fuelled by the arrival of the western pilgrims, but also by his failure to produce a widespread schism among the friends. Through his persistent efforts, however, he created suspicion in the mind of the Válí (Governor) of Beirut, Náẓim Páshá, who communicated false information to Constantinople.

Southern face of the Governorate of 'Abdu'lláh Páshá, showing the main entrance under the archway. The room above the arch witnessed the birth of Shoghi Effendi in March 1897. (c. 1910)

It was in 1901, on the fifth day of the month of Jamádíyu'l-Avval 1319 AH (20 August) that 'Abdu'l-Bahá, upon His return from Bahjí where He had participated in the celebration of the anniversary of the Báb's Declaration, was informed, in the course of an interview with the governor of 'Akká [probably Aḥmad Adíb Bey], of Sulṭán 'Abdu'l-Ḥamíd's instructions ordering that the restrictions which had been gradually relaxed should be reimposed, and that He and His brothers should be strictly confined within the walls of that city. The

Sultán's edict was at first rigidly enforced, the freedom of the exiled community was severely curtailed, while 'Abdu'l-Bahá had to submit, alone and unaided, to the prolonged interrogation of judges and officials, who required His presence for several consecutive days at government headquarters for the purpose of their investigations. One of His first acts was to intercede on behalf of His brothers, who had been peremptorily summoned and informed by the governor of the orders of the sovereign, an act which failed to soften their hostility or lessen their malevolent activities. Subsequently, through His intervention with the civil and military authorities, He succeeded in obtaining the freedom of His followers who resided in 'Akká, and in enabling them to continue to earn, without interference, the means of livelihood. (*God Passes By*, pp. 264–5)

At His table, in those days, whenever there was a lull in the storm raging about Him, there would gather pilgrims, friends and inquirers from most of the aforementioned countries, representative of the Christian, the Muslim, the Jewish, the Zoroastrian, the Hindu and Buddhist Faiths. To the needy thronging His doors and filling the courtyard of His house every Friday morning, in spite of the perils that environed Him, He would distribute alms with His own hands, with a regularity and generosity that won Him the title of 'Father of the Poor'. Nothing in those tempestuous days could shake His confidence, nothing would be allowed to interfere with His ministrations to the destitute, the orphan, the sick, and the downtrodden, nothing could prevent Him from calling in person upon those who were either incapacitated, or ashamed to solicit His aid. Adamant in His determination to follow the example of both the Báb and Bahá'u'lláh, nothing would induce Him to flee from His enemies, or escape from imprisonment . . . So imperturbable was 'Abdu'l-Bahá's equanimity that, while rumours were being bruited about that He might be cast into the sea, or exiled to Fízán in Tripolitania, or hanged on the gallows, He, to the amazement of His friends and the amusement of His enemies, was to be seen planting trees and vines in the garden of His house, whose fruits when the storm had blown over, He would bid His faithful gardener, Ismá'íl Áqá, pluck and present to those same friends and enemies on the occasion of their visits to Him. (ibid. p. 269)

The gravity of the situation confronting 'Abdu'l-Bahá; the rumours that were being set afloat by a population that anticipated the gravest developments; the hints and allusions to the dangers threatening Him contained in newspapers published in Egypt and Syria; the aggressive attitude which His enemies increasingly assumed; the provocative behaviour of some of the inhabitants of 'Akká and Haifa who had been emboldened by the predictions and fabrications of these enemies regarding the fate awaiting a suspected community and its Leader, led Him to reduce the number of pilgrims, and even to suspend, for a time, their visits . . . On certain days and nights, when the outlook was at its darkest, the house in which He was living, and which had for many years been a focus of activity, was completely deserted. Spies, secretly and openly, kept watch around it, observing His every movement and restricting the freedom of His family. (ibid. p. 267)

. . . in the darkest hours of a period which the beloved Guardian describes as 'the most dramatic period of His ministry', 'in the hey-day of His life and in the full tide of His power' He penned the first part of His Will and Testament, which delineates the features and lays the foundations of the Administrative Order to arise after His passing. In this house [of 'Abdu'lláh Páshá] He revealed the highly significant Tablet addressed to the Báb's cousin and chief builder of the 'Ishqábád Temple, a Tablet whose import can be appreciated and grasped only as future events unfold before our eyes, and in which, as testified by Shoghi Effendi, 'Abdu'l-Bahá 'in stirring terms proclaimed the immeasurable greatness of the Revelation of the Báb, sounded the warnings foreshadowing the turmoil which its enemies, both far and near, would let loose upon the world, and prophesied, in moving language, the ascendancy which the torchbearers of the Covenant would ultimately achieve over them.' (*The Bahá'í World*, vol. xvi, p. 104)

During this long period of tension the Master, requiring more and more space for the many needs of His expanding family and the others who came into His charge, also rented the northern buildings of the quadrangle, and there lived the growing families of His daughters. There also were housed Persian pilgrims who came to fulfil their heart's desire to share briefly in the life of the Master.

The Guardian recounts the Master's ceaseless activity and describes the culmination of these very difficult years:

Eyewitnesses have testified that, during that agitated and perilous period of His life, they had known Him to pen, with His own Hand, no less than ninety Tablets in a single day, and to pass many a night, from dusk to dawn, alone in His bedchamber engaged in a correspondence which the pressure of His manifold responsibilities had prevented Him from attending to in the daytime. (*God Passes By*, p. 267)

In the early part of the winter of 1907 another Commission of four officers, headed by 'Árif Bey, and invested with plenary powers, was suddenly dispatched to 'Akká by order of the Sultán. A few days before its arrival 'Abdu'l-Bahá had a dream, which He recounted to the believers, in which He saw a ship cast anchor off 'Akká, from which flew a few birds, resembling sticks of dynamite, and which, circling about His head, as He stood in the midst of a multitude of the frightened inhabitants of the city, returned without exploding to the ship.

No sooner had the members of the Commission landed than they placed under their direct and exclusive control both the Telegraph and Postal services in 'Akká; arbitrarily dismissed officials suspected of being friendly to 'Abdu'l-Bahá, including the governor of the city;[2] established direct and secret contact with the government in Constantinople; took up their residence in the home of the neighbours and intimate associates of the Covenant-breakers;[3] set guards over the house of 'Abdu'l-Bahá to prevent anyone from seeing Him; and started the strange procedure of calling up as witnesses the very people, among whom were Christians and Muslims, orientals and westerners, who had previously signed the documents forwarded to Constantinople, and which they had brought with them for the purpose of their investigations . . .

'Abdu'l-Bahá, while the members of the Commission were carrying on their so-called investigations, and throughout their stay of about one month in 'Akká, consistently refused to meet or have any dealings with any of them, in spite of the veiled threats and warnings conveyed by them to Him through a messenger, an attitude which greatly surprised them and served to inflame their animosity and reinforce their determination to execute their evil designs. Though the perils and tribulations which had encompassed Him were now at their thickest, though the ship on which he was supposed to embark with the members of the Commission was waiting in readiness, at times in 'Akká, at times in Haifa, and the wildest rumours were being spread about Him, the serenity He had invariably maintained, ever since His incarceration had been reimposed, remained unclouded, and His confidence unshaken. 'The meaning of the dream I dreamt', He, at that time, told the believers who still remained in 'Akká, 'is now clear and evident. Please God this dynamite will not explode.'

Meanwhile the members of the Commission had, on a certain Friday, gone to Haifa and inspected the Báb's sepulchre, the construction of which had been proceeding without any interruption on Mt. Carmel. Impressed by its solidity and dimensions, they had inquired of one of the attendants as to the number of vaults that had been built beneath that massive structure.

Shortly after the inspection had been made it was suddenly observed, one day at about sunset, that the ship, which had been lying off Haifa, had weighed anchor, and was heading towards 'Akká. The news spread rapidly among an excited population that the members of the Commission had embarked upon it. It was anticipated that it would stop long enough at 'Akká to take 'Abdu'l-Bahá on board, and then proceed to its destination.

The tent of 'Abdu'l-Bahá, erected in the courtyard of the House of 'Abdu'lláh Páshá. Note the wall of the governorate enclave and the outer sea-wall of the city with gun port. The garden and orchard were planted during His most troubled days. (Chase, 1907)

70

Consternation and anguish seized the members of His family when informed of the approach of the ship. The few believers who were left wept with grief at their impending separation from their Master. 'Abdu'l-Bahá could be seen, at that tragic hour, pacing, alone and silent, the courtyard of His house.

As dusk fell, however, it was suddenly noticed that the lights of the ship had swung round, and the vessel had changed her course. It now became evident that she was sailing direct for Constantinople. The intelligence was instantly communicated to 'Abdu'l-Bahá, Who, in the gathering darkness, was still pacing His courtyard. Some of the believers who had posted themselves at different points to watch the progress of the ship hurried to confirm the joyful tidings. One of the direst perils that had ever threatened 'Abdu'l-Bahá's precious life was, on that historic day, suddenly, providentially and definitely averted.

Soon after the precipitate and wholly unexpected sailing of that ship news was received that a bomb had exploded in the path of the Sulṭán while he was returning to his palace from the mosque where he had been offering his Friday prayers.

A few days after this attempt on his life the Commission submitted its report to him; but he and his government were too preoccupied to consider the matter. The case was laid aside, and when, some months later, it was again brought forward it was abruptly closed forever by an event which, once and for all, placed the Prisoner of 'Akká beyond the power of His royal enemy. The 'Young Turk' Revolution, breaking out swiftly and decisively in 1908, forced a reluctant despot to promulgate the constitution which he had suspended, and to release all religious and political prisoners held under the old régime. Even then a telegram had to be sent to Constantinople to inquire specifically whether 'Abdu'l-Bahá was included in the category of these prisoners, to which an affirmative reply was promptly received. (ibid. pp. 269–72)

The great burden was lifted. With His release by the Young Turks, the Master was free to pursue His immense goals: to develop the nascent Bahá'í World Centre and to greatly expand the Cause in the West and throughout the world.

The Shrine of the Báb on Mount Carmel was completed in its first stage as a simple rectangular building of six rooms. At Naw-Rúz 1909 'Abdu'l-Bahá transported the Holy Dust of the Herald of the Faith from the house in 'Akká to the sacred mountain, and there interred it in the tomb He had so laboriously prepared. (See Chapter 23)

Confidently begun during those troubled years of suspicion and difficulty fomented by the Covenant-breakers, the fine new residence (see Chapter 24) of 'Abdu'l-Bahá was rising at the eastern edge of the German Templer colony in Haifa, at the foot of Mount Carmel and below the Shrine. The time had come to begin in Haifa the creation of a world centre for Bahá'í activities, to develop the Shrine and its surrounding gardens, to acquire new land-holdings on Mount Carmel, and to prepare for the fulfilment of that vision of Bahá'u'lláh revealed in the *Tablet of Carmel*.

The summer house in the south-eastern corner of the courtyard of the House of 'Abdu'lláh Páshá. The western pilgrim is Mrs May Maxwell, the child unidentified. (1909)

With the entombment of the remains of the Báb, the spiritual centre in Haifa came into being, while the Master's removal to Haifa marked the first stage in the upbuilding of the world administrative centre of the Faith. The town of 'Akká henceforth was to become for Bahá'ís a museum of Bahá'í history, echoing with the greatest Words of Bahá'u'lláh's Ministry amid the discord of His great afflictions, fraught too with memories of 'Abdu'l-Bahá's severest challenges, and blessed at being the birthplace of Shoghi Effendi. Before long it would fuse with Haifa as one great metropolis edging the Bay.

The House of 'Abdu'lláh Páshá Restored

From 1910 onwards the house was no longer in Bahá'í hands, but it continued to be a property of the descendants of 'Abdu-'lláh Páshá. For a time during the British Mandate it served as a military hospital. During Israeli days it suffered and deteriorated under various occupants. Then in 1975 the Universal House of Justice cabled to the Bahá'í world:

JOYOUSLY ANNOUNCE SUCCESSFUL CONCLUSION LENGTHY DELICATE NEGOTIATIONS RESULTING ACQUISITION BY PURCHASE HOLY HOUSE CENTRE COVENANT 'ABDU'-L-BAHÁ BIRTHPLACE BELOVED GUARDIAN SHOGHI EFFENDI STOP HISTORIC PROPERTY ADJACENT BARRACKS MOST GREAT PRISON COMPRISES LAND AREA APPROXIMATING SEVEN THOUSAND SQUARE METRES INCLUDES OTHER STRUCTURES WITHIN COMPLEX ASSURING PERMANENT PROTECTION HOUSE VISITED BY MANY PILGRIMS TURN CENTURY SCENE HISTORIC VISIT FIRST GROUP WESTERN PILGRIMS STOP PLANS BEING PREPARED RESTORATION HOLY HOUSE BEAUTIFICATION GROUNDS AS ADDITIONAL PLACE PILGRIMAGE WORLD CENTRE WHEN CIRCUMSTANCES FUNDS PERMIT STOP OFFER HUMBLE THANKSGIVING BAHÁ'U'LLÁH THIS GREAT BLESSING. (*The Bahá'í World*, vol. xvi, p. 103)

For those who visit the house of 'Abdu'lláh Páshá, entry is through the southern and main doorway, through an archway above which lay the room of Shoghi Effendi's birth, passing then down a short hallway into the central courtyard where in 'Abdu'l-Bahá's time was a garden, a well and tall sentinel palm-trees. The stairway to the former Bahá'í living-quarters on the upper floor ascends the inner wall of the western wing to a landing, beyond which is a small roofless court. To the right in the western wing is the small living-room where 'Abdu'l-Bahá met the western pilgrims, and there are also rooms for sleeping and meals, a pantry and a kitchen. The southern wing contains the Master's own room, rooms of some of His daughters and their families, a handsome great hall for family interchanges and, in the south-eastern corner, the room of the Greatest Holy Leaf where the Dust of the Blessed Báb was concealed for a decade. The eastern wing contains rooms occupied or once used by other family members and servants. The ground floor is a place of service rooms and the site of a bath in its western wing.

The northern wing of the quadrangle was built upon extraordinary Crusader fortifications related to the wall of the inner moat of the city. During the years of Bahá'í occupancy, the interconnected buildings provided family housing for the daughters of the Master and for the pilgrims. Still later, many rooms were altered for the use of the mental hospital of the Government of Israel. Now closed as a hospital, the northern wing will soon revert to the Faith. Careful restoration of the entire complex will recall the times when the beloved Master lived and served there.

The Khán-i-'Avámíd (Khán al-'Umdán), looking towards the north-east corner of the hollow square of buildings. The second floor harboured Bahá'í exiles from late 1870 onwards, and rooms in the khán were used by early Bahá'í pilgrims. (1845)

13 The Khán-i-'Avámíd:
the First Pilgrim House

ABOUT 1785 in the south-eastern quarter of 'Akká, Jazzár Páshá had a caravanserai built at the harbour edge, just north of the sea gate and adjacent to the Khán'u'Shúnih of the Crusaders' Pisa Quarter; it is thought by some to have been built on the foundations of a Crusader monastery. The caravanserai was a two-storey building surrounding a square court with fountain, its ground floor comprising warehouse rooms for the storage of goods passing through the port, its upper rooms fitted out for guests. The inner court was marked by a colonnade of heavy granite pillars taken from the ruins of Roman Caesarea, hence its name: Khán-i-'Avámíd, Khán-i-Jurayní, or Khán al-'Umdán – the Inn of the Pillars.[1] The tall clock tower rearing from the northern wing was added in 1906 to commemorate the jubilee of Sultan 'Abdu'l-Ḥamíd II of Turkey.

At the time of the reorganization of the Turkish army in 1869–70, many prisoners were removed from the barracks to detention elsewhere. Bahá'u'lláh and His family were held successively in three private houses, while the majority of the Bahá'ís were consigned to the Khán-i-'Avámíd. There they occupied principally the eastern and southern wings of the upper floor, at first under conditions of deprivation. During the first days of the Bahá'ís' long stay in the khán, food was so scarce that each loaf of Arab bread, normally adequate for one meal for one person, had to be divided into four portions, for the four periods of the day. All other food was strictly divided and assigned; when beans were served, for example, the individual beans were counted and a share allotted to each person.

When the situation of the exiles was gradually ameliorated, a school for the Bahá'í children, including those of the Master, was established at the khán, and they would attend it both mornings and afternoons, learning to read and write. In the square of the inn 'Abdu'l-Bahá is said to have regularly distributed alms to the poor. And it is reported that on certain feast

days the Master was host to the children of 'Akká, offering them refreshments, including sherbet placed in the basin of the fountain.

One of the rooms of the inn was frequently used by the Master, Who there met and greeted guests and pilgrims. For a time Mírzá Músá and his family occupied a small house set inside the courtyard; from here he moved to the house of Malik where Bahá'u'lláh had lived briefly under house arrest. Two rooms were regularly occupied by pilgrims, and the khán was therefore the first pilgrim house in the Holy Land. The pilgrims were welcomed and doubtless prepared for their long-anticipated precious audiences with the Manifestation of God. And of course each group of arrivals brought fresh news of the harried communities in the homeland, where there were recurrent incidents of persecution. When they departed, the pilgrims acted as couriers for Tablets sent by Bahá'u'lláh in which He greatly expanded the believers' knowledge of the Teachings.

The exiles gradually established themselves in shops and homes throughout the city, but some remained in the khán for decades, so that the inn embodies deep memories of the Bahá'í presence. Such eminent early believers as the calligrapher Mishkín-Qalam, the amanuensis Jináb-i-Zayn (Zaynu'l-Muqarrabín), and Hájí Mírzá Haydar-'Alí lived in the caravanserai during the years of Bahá'í occupancy.

Most important of all, the Blessed Beauty Himself visited the khán on His visits to the city during His Bahjí days.

The Khán-i-'Avámíd in the late nineteenth century, during which period some Bahá'ís were still occupants of the upper floor. (École Biblique collection, Jerusalem)

76

14   The Land Gate

AS A KEY PART of the system of fortifications built by Ẓáhiru'l-'Umar, al-Jazzár and Sulaymán, military gateways were constructed at the north-eastern angle of the harbour. In Bahá'u'lláh's day, 'Umar's original 'Lion's Gate' still stood at the site of the *límán* (prison or jail in Turkish). The present gate is that of

The land gate of 'Akká from its vestibule, outer aspect (Welsh, 1921)

The land gate of 'Akká looking outward. Note the massive iron-banded gates. (Welsh, 1921)

al-Jazzár, who built a new wall and moat outside those of 'Umar. At the time of the fort's construction the bay lapped at the foot of the outer walls, and the roadway into the maw of the fortifications led along the edge of the water past the closure of the dry moat. Save for the small sea gate, visible across the harbour, this was then the sole entry into the city.

The gates themselves are massive, of heavy wood sheathed with bolt-studded iron bands, swung on large stone hinges. Their dimensions are respectable: each gate about 5 metres high and almost 2 metres wide. In the western gate at its bottom a small subsidiary door of about 60 cm. square afforded, at times when the gates were closed and bolted, an emergency entry through which, upon opening by the guard, a single person might creep.

The military engineering of the gate was paramount, however, not the comfort nor speed of travel of those passing through the gateway. The direct approach from the east along the beach was commanded by heavy cannon, and also by gun slits for soldiers using small arms. The heavy walls of the gate complex lay, moreover, behind the double row of outer fortifications and the moat. Since the British Mandate, when two new access roads were cut through the walls to create what are now called Haganah and Weizmann Streets, the old land gate into Saladin Street, though functional, has been a museum piece rather than a military obstacle to besiegers.

The gate of course witnessed the passage of Bahá'u'lláh on a number of occasions after His departure for Mazra'ih. It saw innumerable transits of 'Abdu'l-Bahá over the forty-two years of His sojourn in the city, and thereafter through the eight years when He visited 'Akká from His home in Haifa until His passing. And Shoghi Effendi passed its portal very often throughout his life. Hundreds of Persian pilgrims who came during the times of the Prophet and the Master deemed it the gate of fulfilment. Now thousands of Bahá'í pilgrims from around the world see the original land gate, rusted but still formidable, as a memento and symbol of the reality of Bahá'u'lláh's incarceration in that grim prison city which He is now lifting from obscurity to an increasing glory.

The land gate of 'Akká (c. 1840)

79

15 Bahá'í Cemeteries in 'Akká

The Nabí Ṣáliḥ Cemetery

JUST OUTSIDE the eastern limb of the main fortifications of the city, north of the land gate and at the edge of the dry moat which separates the inner and outer lines of the fort, lies a small Muslim cemetery named after one Nabí Ṣáliḥ, of the same name as the holy man mentioned in the Qur'án as a prophet who appeared among the people of Thamúd, and who is also

mentioned by Bahá'u'lláh in *Epistle to the Son of the Wolf*.[1] Near the tomb of this holy man who was considered the patron saint of 'Akká, fourteen Bahá'ís were buried, including the pious Mírzá Mihdí, son of Bahá'u'lláh, whose remains were transferred to Mount Carmel in 1939. For some twelve years the cemetery served the sad purpose of receiving those who, in the arduous early days, were released to the Abhá Kingdom from the privations of the prison city.

The Muslim Cemetery of 'Akká

East of the city near the site of the one-time railway station, now within the area occupied by the Israel School for Naval Officers, a northern part of the extensive Muslim cemetery became after 1880 the burial place of those passing away among the Bahá'í community. This section of the cemetery is now walled and protected from misuse.

In this cemetery lay the remains of the blessed Navváb, Ásíyih Khánum (d. 1886), entitled the Most Exalted Leaf, until her transfer to the Monument Gardens in Haifa. Here was buried the noble Mírzá Músá, Áqáy-i-Kalím (d. 1887), brother of Bahá'u'lláh. Here too was interred Ḥusayn, aged four, the son of 'Abdu'l-Bahá.

In 1892 the poor body of the drowned Nabíl, poet laureate of the Faith at its beginning, a suicide when the sorrow of Bahá'u'lláh's passing became unbearable, was laid here. His own epitaph is poignant:

> Nabíl hath been immersed in the ocean
> of the Mercy of his Glorious Lord.
> Open Thou a way for a consumed heart to see,
> Drowned – drowned in this year let me be!

1310 AH (1892) The Persian word for 'drowned' used here is *gharíq*, and its numerical value is 1310 (i.e. 1892).

About twenty of those whose dust now reposes in this cemetery earned the honour of recognition by 'Abdu'l-Bahá in His book *Memorials of the Faithful*, and are there commemorated for their services to the Cause.

Shrine of Nabí Ṣáliḥ, the patron saint of 'Akká. The iron fence encloses the remaining Bahá'í graves of this cemetery where Mírzá Mihdí was originally buried.

81

Aerial view of 'Akká from the north, with the Tower of the Flies at the new Israeli harbour (top left) and the lighthouse (upper right). Also visible are the Khán-i-'Avámíd (1), the Sinán Mosque (2), Khán-i-Afranj (3), Khán-i-Shávirdí (4), Mosque of al-Jazzár (5), the governorate at the time of Bahá'u'lláh (6), citadel (7), barracks (8), the prison of Bahá'u'lláh (9), House of 'Abdu'lláh Páshá (10), and the House of 'Abbúd (11). (1972)

Aerial photograph of 'Akká peninsula from the south. Note the lighthouse (1), sea gate (2), new breakwater and harbour (3), Khán-i-'Avámíd (4), Khán-i-Afranj (5), Khán-i-Shávirdí (6), fortifications at the land gate (7), al-Jazzár's fortifications and the eastern moat (8), Nabí Ṣáliḥ Cemetery (9), citadel and barracks (10), House of 'Abdu'lláh Páshá (11), and House of 'Abbúd (12).

...erial view of the
...orth-western corner of
...kká, looking
...uth-eastward. Note the
...ll of Bahá'u'lláh in the
...rison (1), the House and
...overnorate of 'Abdu'lláh
...áshá, originally built by
...lí Páshá c. 1810 (2), room
...f the Greatest Holy Leaf
...), room of the birth of
...noghi Effendi (4),
...bdu'l-Bahá's study and
...ception rooms (5), inner
...ourt of the quadrangle (6),
...orthern apartments
...ccupied by Bahá'í families
...nd pilgrims (7), the bath
...rea (8), the Mujádalih
...losque (9), house of the
...overnor on the south-east
...orner of the 'Abdu'lláh
...áshá complex (10), house
...f Shaykh 'Alíy-i-Mírí (11),
...nner moat (12), and the
...estern outer city wall (13).

Photo map of northern
...ection, city of 'Akká. Note
...he cell of Bahá'u'lláh (1),
...vestern section where Holy
...Family was held (2),
...pproximate site of skylight
...ver eastern section (3),
...ections of barracks-prison
...4), citadel (5), barrack-
...quare, formerly a khán (6),
...ormer governorate
...building (7) and its
...courtroom (8), Mosque of
...al-Jazzár (9), madrisih,
...religious school of the
...mosque (10), Sharí'ah
...Court of the 'Akká district
...(11), White Súq of 'Umar
...and Sulaymán (12), inner
...moat, northern defences
...(13), public bath of
...al-Jazzár, now the 'Akká
...Municipal Museum (14).
...(1975)

The 'Akká Area

16 Mazra'ih: Place of Liberation

BAHÁ'U'LLÁH LOVED the beauty and verdure of the country. One day He passed the remark: 'I have not gazed on verdure for nine years. The country is the world of the soul, the city is the world of bodies.' When I heard indirectly of this saying I realized that He was longing for the country, and I was sure that whatever I could do towards the carrying out of His wish would be successful. There was in 'Akká at that time a man called Muḥammad Páshá Ṣafwat,[1] who was very much opposed to us. He had a palace called Mazra'ih,[2] about four miles north of the city, a lovely place, surrounded by gardens and with a stream of running water. I went and called on this Páshá at his home. I said: 'Páshá, you have left the palace empty, and are living in 'Akká.' He replied: 'I am an invalid and cannot leave the city. If I go there it is lonely and I am cut off from my friends.' I said: 'While you are not living there and the place is empty, let it to us.' He was amazed at the proposal, but soon consented. I got the house at a very low rent, about five pounds per annum, paid him for five years and made a contract. I sent labourers to repair the place and put the garden in order and had a bath built. I also had a carriage prepared for the use of the Blessed Beauty. One day I determined to go and see the place for myself. Notwithstanding the repeated injunctions given in successive firmans that we were on no account to pass the limits of the city walls, I walked out through the city gate. Gendarmes were on guard, but they made no objection, so I proceeded straight to the palace. The next day I again went out, with some friends and officials, unmolested and unopposed, although the guards and sentinels stood on both sides of the City Gates. Another day I arranged a banquet, spread a table under the pine trees of Bahjí, and gathered round it the notables and officials of the town. In the evening we all returned to the town together.

One day I went to the Holy Presence of the Blessed Beauty and said: 'The palace at Mazra'ih is ready for you, and a carriage to drive you there.' (At that time there were no carriages in 'Akká or Haifa.) He refused to go, saying: 'I am a prisoner.' Later I requested Him again, but got the same answer. I went so far as to ask Him a third time, but he still said 'No!' and I did not dare to insist further. There was, however, in 'Akká a certain Muḥammadan Shaykh,[3] a well-known man with considerable influence, who loved Bahá'u'lláh and was greatly favoured by Him. I called this Shaykh and explained the

The staircase at Mazra'ih, leading from the tower base to the upper floor

position to him. I said, 'You are daring. Go tonight to His Holy Presence, fall on your knees before Him, take hold of His hands and do not let go until He promises to leave the city!' He was an Arab . . . He went directly to Bahá'u'lláh and sat down close to His knees. He took hold of the hands of the Blessed Beauty and kissed them and asked: 'Why do you not leave the city?' He said: 'I am a prisoner.' The Shaykh replied: 'God forbid! Who has the power to make you a prisoner? You have kept yourself in prison. It was your own will to be imprisoned, and now I beg you to come out and go to the palace. It is beautiful and verdant. The trees are lovely, and the oranges like balls of fire!' As often as the Blessed Beauty said: 'I am a prisoner, it cannot be,' the Shaykh took His hands and kissed them. For a whole hour he kept on pleading. At last Bahá'u'lláh said, 'Khaylí Khub (very good)' and the Shaykh's patience and persistence were rewarded. He came to me with great joy to give the glad news of His Holiness's consent. In spite of the strict firman of 'Abdu'l-'Azíz which prohibited my meeting or having any intercourse with the Blessed Perfection, I took the carriage the next day and drove with Him to the palace. No one made any objection. I left Him there and returned myself to the city. (Words of 'Abdu'l-Bahá quoted in Esslemont, *Bahá'u'lláh and the New Era*, pp. 48–50)

Nabíl records that Bahá'u'lláh's liberation occurred in the early days of June 1877.[4] His departure from the prison city marks the termination of His confinement and the opening of a brief but rewarding two years of His life.

The Mansion of Mazra'ih at the turn of the century. Note that Bahá'u'lláh's room, at the upper left, then had three windows, and the western ground-floor rooms had not yet been added. (Getsinger, *c.* 1900)

The summer mansion of 'Abdu'lláh Páshá at Mazra'ih to which He now repaired was of a simple design. The rectangular stone building was set in gardens, its finest view eastward to the Galilee hills across a terrace, the aqueduct, a pool[5] and wide fields, but also it faced northward into a large walled garden with bath and service buildings, southward into open gardens, and westward to the sea a half-mile distant. A square tower with archways formed an entrance on the north-west corner; once this may have been the formal entryway for carriages. One arch opened to an outside stairway rising to a small landing with balcony on the upper floor and roof. On the ground floor were two large rooms, the eastern one of which Bahá'u'lláh used as His audience chamber and as His favoured place for dictation of Tablets. On the upper level the tower room was His, a place of light and air and of views to the sea and the hills. Mazra'ih was, in short, a place of beauty, the place where the Spirit of Bahá'u'lláh returned to the countryside He had cherished from His days in the mountains of Mázindarán.

Because of the limited space in the house, the Blessed Beauty went to Mazra'ih with members of His family, and accompanied by Mírzá Áqá Ján, Khádimu'lláh, His amanuensis. A frequent visitor was the Master, and the Greatest Holy Leaf,

Aerial view of the Mansion of Mazra'ih and its environs, looking westward to the sea. Note the Mansion, its gardens and eastern pool, the aqueduct of Kabrí at the left, and the old caravanserai in the centre. (1975)

His esteemed daughter, also often came. Muḥammad Khán, a Balúchí, was Bahá'u'lláh's faithful doorkeeper. At intervals He returned to 'Akká for visits.

During the two years of His sojourn at Mazra'ih the pilgrims continued to arrive, to pay homage to Him even though serious repressions were upon them in Persia. One who came during this period was Ḥájí Muḥammad Ṭáhir-i-Málmírí,[6] who was allowed to remain for nine months, during which time he had a number of interviews with Bahá'u'lláh. He has recorded that he could never look directly at Him, nor when in His Presence could he remember the questions he had carefully prepared; nevertheless, Bahá'u'lláh answered the forgotten questions. Another pilgrim, Ḥájí Mullá Mihdíy-i-Yazdí[7] of Ṭihrán, arrived in the village of Mazra'ih gravely ill, and passed away some time between 15 and 26 December 1878, before he glimpsed his Lord; his grave in the village cemetery is mute tribute to his unfulfilled aspiration.

During the two years at Mazra'ih Bahá'u'lláh sent forth numerous Tablets to individuals, committing them to the

Bahá'u'lláh's spacious room on the ground floor of the Mansion of Mazra'ih; here He met His guests and dictated to His amanuenses. The windows at the left look to the Galilee hills, those at the right into the southern gardens.

hands of trusted Bahá'ís for delivery. This was a period in Persia marked by savage attacks upon the believers; nevertheless, stimulated by the guidance from the Holy Land, they continued to engage in active propagation of the Faith. In Iṣfahán in February and March of 1879 there had occurred the violent martyrdoms of Mullá Kázim and of 'the two famous brothers Mírzá Muḥammad-Ḥasan and Mírzá Muḥammad-Ḥusayn, the "twin shining lights", respectively surnamed "Sulṭánu'sh-Shuhadá" (King of Martyrs) and "Maḥbúbu'sh-Shuhadá" (Beloved of Martyrs), who were celebrated for their generosity, trustworthiness, kindliness and piety'. In sharp response to these monstrous acts Bahá'u'lláh revealed the *Lawḥ-i-Burhán*, the Tablet of the Proof, in which 'the acts perpetrated by Shaykh Muḥammad-Báqir, surnamed "Dhi'b" (Wolf), and Mír Muḥammad-Ḥusayn, the Imám-Jum'ih of Iṣfáhán, surnamed "Raqshá" (She-Serpent), are severely condemned . . .' (*God Passes By*, pp. 200 and 219)

In the summer of 1879 there occurred one of those natural disasters for which 'Akká was the frequent host: an epidemic of plague[8] erupted. As was their wont, those who could do so wisely fled from the centre of the epidemic; included among those who abandoned the city and its environs were 'Údí Khammár and his family. 'Abdu'l-Bahá relates its consequences for Bahá'u'lláh:

It so happened that an epidemic disease had broken out at Bahjí, and the proprietor of the house fled away in distress, with all his family, ready to offer the house free of charge to any applicant. We took the house at a very low rent, and there the doors of majesty and true sovereignty were flung wide open. (Esslemont, *supra*, p. 50)

Mazra'ih in its Later Years

The House remained in the possession of the descendants of Muḥammad Ṣafwat during the period of the British Mandate. Then, in about 1928, Mrs Lilian McNeill came to the Holy Land with her husband, a Brigadier-General who had been with Allenby in the conquest of Palestine. Mrs McNeill had been a childhood friend in Malta of the English princess who became Queen Marie of Rumania.[9] She relates that when she

Col. Aḥmad Jarráḥ, commander of the guard during and after Bahá'u'lláh's incarceration in the prison of 'Akká. This portrait hangs at the foot of the great stairs at Mazra'ih. (1870s)

was making a journey of discovery in the area below Nahariya and travelling

. . . across country where then only the roughest of tracks existed, I came upon an old house, neglected, some parts almost ruinous. Two gigantic cypress trees, said to be hundreds of years old, stand sentinel beside it. An inside courtyard surrounded by a thick, high wall. Outside a little paved terrace through which flows the aqueduct which supplies the orange gardens and the town of Akka, and steps leading down to further terraces of gardens. There was a Bedouin family living in a tent in the garden, and the olive pickers from a village near Carmel had been allowed to live in the lower floor of the house three winters running during the olive harvest, so the state of the place can be imagined!

Nevertheless I saw the possibilities and the poor old house with its vaulted lower rooms had an intense and almost weird fascination for me.

Soon the mansion of Mazra'ih came back into the hands of a Bahá'í, for, as Mrs McNeill records it:

It was in May, 1931 when my husband retired from Government service that we took a lease of this house and it was our great privilege to be able to restore it, and make a garden – a proper setting for a dwelling with such sacred associations. Although we found it a good deal altered on the second floor from the time when Bahá'u'lláh lived there, the main features are unchanged, the vaulted rooms on the ground floor particularly.

Mazra'ih seen from the south during the McNeill occupancy (early 1930s)

The Mansion of Mazra'ih
from the west

There is a rough cement floor in the room downstairs which was Bahá'u'lláh's own special room. This remains as I found it, in the belief that His feet may have trodden it . . . (See Bibliography)

Mrs McNeill and Queen Marie hoped for a reunion in Palestine in 1938, but the Queen's ill health and the unsettled state of the country made it impossible. After this disappointment Queen Marie wrote to her friend, 'It was indeed nice to hear from you, and to think that you are of all things living near Haifa and are, as I am, a follower of the Bahá'í teachings. It interests me that you are living in that special house . . . I was so intensely interested and studied each photo intently. It must be a lovely place . . . and the house you live in, so incredibly attractive and made precious by its associations with the Man we all venerate . . .' (*God Passes By*, p. 393)

Mrs McNeill passed away in 1947, her husband later moving to Cyprus. In December 1950, through the Guardian's direct appeal to the Prime Minister, David Ben-Gurion, the Bahá'í interest in the property as a Holy Place was recognized by the Government of Israel, and he was able to lease the property, joyfully cabling to the Bahá'í world, 15 December 1950:

93

ANNOUNCE FRIENDS DELIVERY AFTER MORE THAN FIFTY YEARS KEYS QASR MAZRA'IH BY ISRAEL AUTHORITIES STOP HISTORIC DWELLING PLACE BAHÁ'U'LLÁH AFTER LEAVING PRISON CITY 'AKKÁ NOW BEING FURNISHED ANTICIPATION OPENING DOOR PILGRIMAGE.

In March 1973 the Universal House of Justice cabled further good news: 'OCCASION NAWRÚZ 130 JOYOUSLY ANNOUNCE BAHÁ'Í WORLD ACQUISITION BY PURCHASE MANSION MAZRA'IH.' It was acquired from a descendant of 'Abdu'lláh Páshá, thereby adding immeasurably to the Bahá'í endowments in the Holy Land. And in September 1980 land at the north-eastern corner of the Mansion was purchased to provide additional garden space, as recorded in a cablegram:

PURCHASED NEARLY 50,000 SQUARE METRES AGRICULTURAL LAND ADJACENT TO AND NORTH OF MAZRA'IH PROPERTY AS PROTECTION TO MANSION IN RAPIDLY DEVELOPING AREA. (24 September)

The Mansion of Mazra'ih, view north-eastward from the gardens to the Galilee hills; the room of Bahá'u'lláh is on the extreme left, upper floor. (1975)

17　The Riḍván Garden

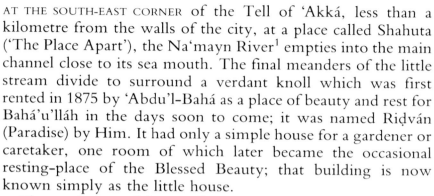

AT THE SOUTH-EAST CORNER of the Tell of 'Akká, less than a kilometre from the walls of the city, at a place called Shahuta ('The Place Apart'), the Na'mayn River[1] empties into the main channel close to its sea mouth. The final meanders of the little stream divide to surround a verdant knoll which was first rented in 1875 by 'Abdu'l-Bahá as a place of beauty and rest for Bahá'u'lláh in the days soon to come; it was named Riḍván (Paradise) by Him. It had only a simple house for a gardener or caretaker, one room of which later became the occasional resting-place of the Blessed Beauty; that building is now known simply as the little house.

The little house where Bahá'u'lláh rested during His visits to the Riḍván Garden

The garden possibly was first visited by Bahá'u'lláh in June 1877 during the period when He was leaving the prison city and transferring His residence to Mazra'ih. Thereafter it became a spot enjoying His frequent visits, for it was well loved by Him, and in 1881 was purchased in His name. Shoghi Effendi succinctly described this garden in relation to the prison city:

The garden of Na'mayn, a small island, situated in the middle of a river to the east of the city, honoured with the appellation of Riḍván, and designated by Him the 'New Jerusalem' and 'Our Verdant Isle', had, together with the residence of 'Abdu'lláh Páshá, – rented and prepared for Him by 'Abdu'l-Bahá, and situated a few miles north of 'Akká – become by now the favourite retreats of One Who, for almost a decade, had not set foot beyond the city walls, and Whose sole exercise had been to pace, in monotonous repetition, the floor of His bed-chamber. (*God Passes By*, p. 193)

Lady Blomfield has given an attractive description of the garden and the pilgrims who beautified it:

The Riḍván is a beautiful garden, which the Master had planted in a plot of land which He had acquired. It is on the bank of a brook. There is a large mulberry tree with seats round its trunk. Many beautiful blossoming trees are now flourishing there, also flowers innumerable, and sweet-smelling herbs; it is a blaze of glorious colour and wonderful beauty. The scent of attar roses, of rosemary, bergamot, mint and thyme and balm, lemon-scented verbena, and musk makes the air sweet with their wealth of various fragrances. Scented white and scarlet and rose-coloured geraniums are there in wild luxuriance, and trees of pomegranate with their large, brilliant scarlet blossoms, also other lovely blooming shrubs. Each a symbol of devoted, loving service.

Most of the flowering plants have been brought from Persia by the pilgrims.

These wonderful pilgrims! How they came on that long, toilsome journey on foot, braving numberless dangers, malignant human enemies and bad weather, and through all the fatigue, carrying, as the greatest treasure, some plant for their adored one's garden. Often the only water, which the devoted pilgrims so urgently needed for themselves, was given to the plant.

Some of the gardeners who had been in the employ of Bahá'u'lláh in His glorious gardens at the beautiful country house, His former home in Persia, remembered that a particular white rose was a favourite flower of Bahá'u'lláh's. This rose, single with golden centre, brownish stalks, shiny leaves, and a peculiarly delightful scent, is now flourishing in the Riḍván. Many bushes of these beautiful roses are in full bloom; the waxen cream and gold of their blossoms, and their burnished leaves, make a pure and peaceful note in the love-laden harmony of the glory of that garden. (*The Chosen Highway*, p. 96)

Ṭúbá Khánum, one of the daughters of 'Abdu'l-Bahá, recalled the appeal of the garden, and its singular qualities as remembered from her childhood:

Oh the joy of the day when Bahá'u'lláh went to the beautiful Riḍván, which had been prepared for Him with such loving care by the Master, the friends, and the pilgrims!

The Master's heart was gladdened indeed to see the enjoyment of His beloved Father, resting under the big mulberry tree, by the side of the little river rippling by, the fountain which they had contrived splashing and gurgling in sounds refreshing indeed after the long years of confinement in the pestilential air of the penal fortress of 'Akká. Only those who were present there could realize in any degree what it meant to be surrounded by such profusion of flowers, their colours and their scents, after the dull walls and unfragrant odours of the prison city. (ibid. p. 97)

Not only was the garden a place of rest and relaxation for Bahá'u'lláh from the daily cares of His household and the

The Riḍván Garden, showing the two old mulberry trees within the rectangle of benches at the garden's centre, and the spot where Bahá'u'lláh customarily sat at the right. (Thornton Chase, 1907)

pilgrims who thronged Bahjí, and from His interminable correspondence which instructed and strengthened the friends, but it was also a Place of Revelation. As Bahá'u'lláh relates in the Fourth Ṭaráz of the Tablet of Ṭarázát:

Not long ago these sublime words were revealed from the Pen of the Most High:

'We will now mention unto thee Trustworthiness and the station thereof in the estimation of God, thy Lord, the Lord of the Mighty Throne. One day of days We repaired unto Our Green Island. Upon Our arrival, We beheld its streams flowing, and its trees luxuriant, and the sunlight playing in their midst. Turning Our face to the right, We beheld what the pen is powerless to describe; nor can it set forth that which the eye of the Lord of Mankind witnessed in that most sanctified, that most sublime, that blest, and most exalted Spot. Turning, then, to the left We gazed on one of the Beauties of the Most Sublime Paradise, standing on a pillar of light, and calling aloud saying: "O inmates of earth and heaven! Behold ye My beauty, and My radiance, and My revelation, and My effulgence. By God, the True One! I am Trustworthiness and the revelation thereof, and the beauty thereof. I will recompense whosoever will cleave unto Me, and recognize My rank and station, and hold fast unto My hem. I am the most great ornament of the people of Bahá, and the vesture of glory unto all who are in the kingdom of creation. I am the supreme instrument for the prosperity of the world, and the horizon of assurance unto all beings." Thus have We sent down for thee that which will draw men nigh unto the Lord of creation.'

O people of Bahá! Trustworthiness is in truth the best of vestures for your temples and the most glorious crown for your heads. Take ye fast hold of it at the behest of Him Who is the Ordainer, the All-Informed. (*Tablets of Bahá'u'lláh*, pp. 37–8)

Gateway to the Riḍván
Garden which lies at the left
across a small bridge.
(Baker, early 1930s)

The fountain in the centre
of the Riḍván Garden,
'splashing and gurgling' its
way to the pools back of the
benches. (Baker, early
1930s)

A Tablet, now framed and hanging in Bahá'u'lláh's room in the little house, tells of the spirit which pervaded events at this blessed Spot, and also of a specific time and happening at the garden. It was addressed to the husband of Rádíyih.

He is God, Glorified be He,
Grandeur and Might are His!

On the morning of the blessed Friday we proceeded from the Mansion and entered the Garden. Every tree uttered a word, and every leaf sang a melody. The trees proclaimed: 'Behold the evidences of God's Mercy' and the twin streams recited in the eloquent tongue the sacred verse 'From us all things were made alive'. Glorified be God! Mysteries were voiced by them, which provoked wonderment. Methought: in which school were they educated, and from whose presence had they acquired their learning? Yea! This Wronged One knoweth and He saith: 'From God, the All-Encompassing, the Self-Subsistent.'

Upon Our being seated, Rádíyih, upon her be My glory, attained Our presence on thy behalf, laid the table of God's bounty and in thy name extended hospitality to all present. In truth, all that which stimulateth the appetite and pleaseth the eye was offered, and indeed that which delighteth the ear could also be heard as the leaves were stirred by the Will of God, and from this movement a refreshing voice was raised, as if uttering a blissful call inviting the absent to this Feast. God's power and the perfection of His handiwork could enjoyably be seen in the blossoms, the fruits, the trees, the leaves and the streams. Praised be God Who hath thus confirmed thee and her.

In brief, all in the Garden were recipients of the choicest bounties and in the end expressed their thanksgiving unto their Lord. O that all God's beloved would have been present on this day!

We beseech God, exalted be He, to cause to descend upon thee at every moment, a blessing and a mercy and a measure of divine grace from His presence. He is the Forgiving, the All-Glorious.

We send greetings to His loved ones, and supplicate for each one of them that which is worthy of mention and is acceptable in His presence. Peace be upon thee, and upon God's sincere servants. Praise be to Him, the Lord of all mankind.

The memories of His granddaughter Ṭúbá bring us close to the joy of the hours spent by Bahá'u'lláh at the Garden:

I remember well the greatest of our joys was to go with Bahá'u'lláh for the occasional picnics to the Riḍván . . . How we adored Him!

'Now children, tomorrow you shall come with Me for a picnic to the Riḍván,' He would say, and our night was so full of joy we could scarcely sleep. (*The Chosen Highway*, pp. 97–8)

The Riḍván Garden was a place of happy spirit reflecting the Blessed Beauty's love of the out-of-doors, for throughout His long life He felt the country to be the place of the spirit, the city the world of material things.

During one Riḍván period Bahá'u'lláh sojourned there for nine days and nights, meeting pilgrim groups who came out from 'Akká each day to be in His presence.

The little house in the Riḍván Garden. The doorway to the room where Bahá'u'lláh used to rest opens to the right of the young man in the black coat. Note the little stream flowing past the house, with its water-gate and steps. (Getsinger, *c.* 1900)

Many and heart-warming are the stories associated with the garden, with the Master and the believers who were its frequenters, with the gardeners, the custodians and the pilgrims who brought their rose bushes, their jasmine, their precious plants from distant Persia. Peacocks once roamed the gardens, but are now confined to pens. A succession of devoted gardeners have laboured to bring the rich earth to its present beauty. The original mulberry trees whose branches overhung the benches of the mid-garden grew strongly, producing a wondrous deep shade; the last one succumbed only in 1977, having in its last years appropriately become a bee tree and storage spot for honey. Two sturdy successor mulberry trees provide the same deep shade. The water fountain has, from Bahá'u'lláh's time to this, delivered abundant purling waters from its basin through the garden channel to the eastern pools, now filled to become orchards.

In recent years the drainage of the Na'mayn swamps, the diversion of the stream's waters by the British and the Israelis, and the effects of malaria control and water utilization programmes have produced a drying up of the encircling watercourses and of the garden's wells which once were its water supply.

The Riḍván Garden area

From the earliest times of settlement upon the Tell of 'Akká, when the Canaanite–Phoenician[2] city of Accho was a bustling lively small port serving the hinterland of ancient Syria, far-

The heart of the Riḍván Garden, with the bench shown where Bahá'u'lláh sat under the mulberry trees, leafless in this winter photograph. In the background are remnants of the old mill whose pools are seen as a shimmer behind the benches. (c. 1923)

mers doubtless struggled to till the fertile but swampy lands at the mouth of the nearby little river which drained a large part of the hills of western Galilee. In later times the stream was known to the Greeks and Romans as the Belus, and Pliny, the Roman historian, has it that near here occurred the great discovery of how to produce glass from silicon, sand and soda (natron). In still later Arab centuries it was renamed the Na'mayn.

In Roman times, when a new suburb of the city had been established and named Colonia Claudio Felix Ptolemais (see p. 17), it is thought that this settlement of invalided Roman legionaries may have been sited at the south-east edge of Ptolemais in a spot suitable for farming and for work in the city and port, in short in the area where now lie the Bahá'í Riḍván, Ashraf and Firdaws Gardens.

The house of the custodians of the Firdaws Garden. Bahá'u'lláh once pitched His tent close by, and on occasion 'Abdu'l-Bahá rested in the upper room.

During the two centuries when the Crusaders occupied Acre, as they called it, the Knights of St. John of the Hospital are thought to have been responsible for construction of a water-mill whose ruins lie on the south-east edge of the Riḍván Garden. Water from the Na'mayn was impounded in long parallel pools just east of the garden knoll, pools still in existence at the time of Bahá'u'lláh. The mill building stood southeast of the present little house; here water was channelled through sluices to turn grinding-stones on the floor above, an ingenious device, and was finally spilled into a canal emptying into the nearby Na'mayn.

The Firdaws and Ashraf Gardens

Immediately adjacent to the Riḍván Garden and beyond the little stream which marks its western boundary lie two large gardens; one was named the Firdaws (Paradise) Garden, the other the 'Alí-Ashraf Garden, after its former owner.

The Firdaws Garden covers an extensive agricultural area, with the house of the former gardener-custodians – Jamshíd and his brother Húshang, whose family now bears the name Firdawsí – situated at the north-west corner, near the well and its storage pool which then supplied water for irrigation, and even for swimming. In that garden near the pool Bahá'u'lláh once pitched His tent. In 1881 the garden was purchased in the name of Bahá'u'lláh at the same time as the Riḍván Garden's acquisition. Later 'Abdu'l-Bahá had a small room built atop the house for His use, and there on occasion He rested during His visits.

The Ashraf Garden area was bought originally by Mullá

Aerial view of the Riḍván, Ashraf and Firdaws Gardens east of 'Akká. In the Riḍván Garden (1) note the little house (2), in the Ashraf Garden (3) the house of the custodians of the Garden (4), and in the Firdaws Garden (5) the house where the Master sometimes stayed (6), near the site where Bahá'u'lláh pitched His tent. (1967)

The water-lift of the Garden of Firdaws: a well used to irrigate the fertile lands adjacent to Tell 'Akká and the Riḍván Garden; the edge of its reservoir seen lower left. (Welsh, 1921)

Abú-Ṭálib, a master mason who, before the passing of Bahá'u'lláh, came to the Holy Land from Bakú in Russia with his two sons 'Alí-Ashraf and Abú-Báláh. He had original responsibility for construction of the Shrine of the Báb under the Master's supervision and two doors of the Shrine are named for his sons. Abú-Ṭálib gave the property to his son 'Alí-Ashraf, who later donated it to the Faith. The present custodians live on this property not far from the little house, providing care for the approximately 19½ acres (78 dunams) of the three gardens.

The Shrine of Bahá'u'lláh and the Mansion of Bahjí looking eastward from the pine grove. In the foreground note the thin line of masonry, with people standing upon it, which marks the aqueduct of Sulaymán. (Baker, early 1930s)

18 Bahjí: Days of Glory and Revelation

PLEASANT AND PRODUCTIVE as were the two years at the Mansion of Mazra'ih, it was far too small to serve the many needs of the Blessed Beauty, the Holy Family, and the expanding company of exiles and expatriate settlers in 'Akká. Thus it was timely when, in 1879,

. . . the palace of 'Údí Khammár, on the construction of which so much wealth had been lavished, while Bahá'u'lláh lay imprisoned in the barracks, and which its owner had precipitately abandoned with his family owing to the outbreak of an epidemic disease, was rented and later purchased for Him – a dwelling-place which He characterized as the 'lofty mansion', the spot which 'God hath ordained as the most sublime vision of mankind'. (*God Passes By*, p. 193)

The doorway of the Mansion of Bahjí, situated at the north-eastern corner. (*Insert*) The dedicatory statement of 'Údí Khammár, placed over the lintel upon completion of the mansion's restoration in 1870.

It was indeed a far more befitting home for the High Prophet during the final chapter of His momentous human existence, for 'Údí Khammár's commercial successes had allowed him to add extensively to the original structure built in 1821 by 'Abdu'lláh Páshá for his mother. The mansion was surrounded by a garden and high wall; the subsidiary houses and buildings once occupied by 'Údí Khammár's relatives lay outside. The land on which it was built was situated just north of the estate and great country house of Sulaymán Páshá and 'Abdu'lláh Páshá.[1] The aqueduct from Kabrí crossed Jamál land near the 'Údí Khammár property at ground level and continued southward to 'Akká past the Páshás' mansion, gardens, pool and orchards; the area round about was known as al-Bahja, Place of Delight. Who can now know what thoughts impelled 'Údí Khammár, when his mansion was finished in 1870, to place over the main doorway an inscription in Arabic which welcomed visitors with a great promise:

> Greetings and salutations rest upon this Mansion which increaseth in splendour through the passage of time. Manifold wonders and marvels are found therein, and pens are baffled in attempting to describe them.[2]

With Bahá'u'lláh's coming the Mansion of Bahjí met its destiny. The Bahá'í families which came to Bahjí occupied the buildings surrounding the Mansion and a part of the Mansion itself, living simply, joyfully aware of the new bounties of freedom. Bahá'u'lláh Himself lived in utmost simplicity, surrounded by family, disciples and pilgrims, and seeing occasional visitors.

Tablets and letters flowed from the Pen of the Prophet. Shaykh Salmán and other couriers came from 'Iráq or Persia, returning to deliver to individuals and communities messages which, in part, had been stimulated by the acute needs of the believers, their heroism and sacrifices during the persecutions of the 1880s in Bahá'u'lláh's native land. His amanuensis was Mírzá Áqá Ján. Zaynu'l-Muqarrabín and others were engaged in the labour of transcribing dictated letters and Tablets, illuminating existing Tablets, and copying the Writings of Bahá'u'lláh for want of printing facilities. And meanwhile Nabíl worked on his monumental collection of original historical materials describing the origins of the Faith.

The pilgrims were given audience by the Prophet in His room at the south-eastern corner of the Mansion on the upper floor, often after preparatory reception and welcome by the Master in 'Akká. Many are the personal recollections of this memorable period when many lives were touched and confirmed.[3] Indeed, Bahá'u'lláh Himself said of this time at

Bahjí: 'Verily, verily, the most wretched prison has been converted into a Paradise of Eden.'

During the years immediately following the revelation of the *Kitáb-i-Aqdas* and its appendix, the *Questions and Answers*, there occurred a ceaseless outflow of Bahá'u'lláh's Writings,

The Mansion of Bahjí

recorded in unnumbered Tablets, which He continued to reveal until the last days of His earthly life, among which the *Ishráqát* (Splendours), the *Bishárát* (Glad Tidings), the *Ṭarázát* (Ornaments), the *Tajallíyát* (Effulgences), the *Kalimát-i-Firdawsíyyih* (Words of Paradise), the *Lawh-i-Aqdas* (Most Holy Tablet), the *Lawh-i-Dunyá* (Tablet of the World), the *Lawh-i-Maqṣúd* (Tablet of Maqsúd), are the most noteworthy. These Tablets – mighty and final effusions of His indefatigable pen – must rank among the choicest fruits which His mind has yielded, and mark the consummation of His forty-year-long ministry. (*God Passes By*, p. 216)

In 1891 He penned the final great work of His Ministry, the *Epistle to the Son of the Wolf*, a fresh expression of many of His most potent passages, but also containing much original content. It was addressed to Shaykh Muḥammad Taqíy-i-Najafí, vicious in his own right as the murderer of Mírzá Ashraf in 1888, and well prepared for his villainies by his father (the Wolf), so stigmatized by Bahá'u'lláh for the murders of the King of Martyrs and the Beloved of Martyrs.

During these last years of His life, Bahá'u'lláh was free to explore the nearby environs of His place of 'perpetual banishment'. Occasionally He repaired to the Garden of Junaynih, near Mazra'ih, an extensive property owned by several of the Bahá'ís. Often He visited the Garden of Riḍván, and once pitched His tent in the adjacent Firdaws Garden. He undertook His several journeys to visit the friendly Druze of Abú-Sinán and Yirkih (Yerka). He enjoyed the cool beauty of the Garden of 'Afífí, near the springs of Kabrí. A number of times He returned to 'Akká: to the houses of the Master (the House of 'Abbúd), His brothers Mírzá Músá and Mírzá Muḥammad-Qulí, and of Bahá'í families living in the Súq al-Abyad and in the small Jewish quarter; to the Khán-i-Afranj and the Khán-i-'Avámíd with their many Bahá'í families; and twice He visited the mound of the ancient city of 'Akká. In His visits to 'Akká He stayed in or visited three other houses.

At one time, during His stay in the barracks, Bahá'u'lláh had written: 'Fear not. These doors shall be opened. My tent shall be pitched on Mount Carmel, and the utmost joy shall be realized.' (Esslemont, *Bahá'u'lláh and the New Era*, p. 48) In fulfilment of His prediction, He travelled three times to Haifa; He is known to have been there in August 1883, in April 1890, and again in the summer of 1891 for three months, visits of the greatest importance, for during the last of these occurred His choice of the site of the Shrine of the Báb, and the revelation of the *Tablet of Carmel* near the site of the future Mashriqu'l-Adhkár of the World Centre. During those three visits He also once pitched His tent where the Western Pilgrim House now stands (present-day No. 10 Haparsim Street), and once at the base of Mount Carmel at the edge of the German Templer colony, and for brief periods He occupied rooms of the Templer inn and certain known houses in that colony.

During this period

Men of letters, and even 'ulamás residing in Syria, were moved, as the years rolled by, to voice their recognition of Bahá'u'lláh's rising greatness and power. 'Azíz Páshá, who, in Adrianople, had evinced a profound attachment to 'Abdu'l-Bahá, and had in the meantime been promoted to the rank of Válí, twice visited 'Akká for the express purpose of paying his respects to Bahá'u'lláh, and to renew his friendship with One Whom he had learned to admire and revere. (*God Passes By*, p. 192)

During these fruitful years, Bahá'u'lláh chose at least four distinguished believers noted for their piety, their learning, their loyalty and their intense spirit, calling them in His letters 'Hands of the Cause of God'. The noble four thus confirmed were Ḥájí Mullá 'Alí-Akbar-i-Shahmírzádí, known as Ḥájí Ákhúnd;[4] Ḥájí Mírzá Muḥammad Taqíy-i-Abharí, known as Ibn-i-Abhar; Mírzá Muḥammad-Ḥasan, entitled Adíbu'l-'Ulamá, known as Adíb (the Learned One); and Mírzá 'Alí-Muḥammad, known as Ibn-i-Aṣdaq (the True One).

In April 1890 there arrived Edward Granville Browne, an English orientalist from Cambridge University who, fascinated by the Bábí religion and its evolution into the Bahá'í Faith under Bahá'u'lláh, sought the source of the new religious phenomenon. His fluency in Persian and Arabic, as well as his intensive preparation for the unique visit, singularly fitted him for his memorable days in the Holy Land and at Bahjí. The climactic event of Browne's five-day sojourn at Bahjí was when he was conducted to the room of Bahá'u'lláh at the south-eastern corner of the Mansion. His historic description of that first interview with the High Prophet reflects his sensitivity and keen observation.

. . . my conductor paused for a moment while I removed my shoes. Then with a quick movement of the hand he withdrew, and, as I passed, replaced the curtain; and I found myself in a large apartment, along the upper end of which ran a low divan, while on the side opposite to the door were placed two or three chairs. Though I dimly suspected whither I was going, and whom I was to behold (for no distinct intimation had been given to me), a second or two elapsed ere, with a throb of wonder and awe, I became definitely conscious that the room was not untenanted. In the corner where the divan met the wall sat a wondrous and venerable figure, crowned with a felt head-dress of the kind called táj by dervishes (but of unusual height and make), round the base of which was wound a small white turban. The face of him on whom I gazed I can never forget, though I cannot describe it. Those piercing eyes seemed to read one's very soul; power and authority sat on that ample brow; while the deep lines on the forehead and face implied an age which the jet-black hair and beard flowing down in indistinguishable luxuriance almost to the waist seemed to belie. No need to ask in whose presence I stood, as I bowed myself before One who is the object of a devotion and love which kings might envy and emperors sigh for in vain!

The Mansion of Bahjí, south-western corner of the balcony

A mild dignified voice bade me be seated, and then continued: 'Praise be to God that thou hast attained! . . . Thou hast come to see a prisoner and an exile. . . . We desire but the good of the world and the happiness of the nations; yet they deem us a stirrer-up of strife and sedition worthy of bondage and banishment. . . . That all nations should become one in faith and all men as brothers; that the bonds of affection and unity between the sons of men should be strengthened; that diversity of religion should cease, and differences of race be annulled—what harm is there in this? . . . Yet so it shall be; these fruitless strifes, these ruinous wars shall pass away, and the "Most Great Peace" shall come . . . Do not you in Europe need this also? Is not this that which Christ foretold? . . . Yet do we see your kings and rulers lavishing their treasures more freely on means for the destruction of the human race than on that which would conduce to the happiness of mankind. . . . These strifes and this bloodshed and discord must cease, and all men be as one kindred and one family. . . . Let not a man glory in this, that he loves his country; let him rather glory in this, that he loves his kind. . . .'

Such, so far as I can recall them, were the words which, besides many others, I heard from Bahá. Let those who read them consider well with themselves whether such doctrines merit death and bonds, and whether the world is more likely to gain or lose by their diffusion. (Browne, *A Traveller's Narrative*, vol. ii, xxxix-xl)

The Passing of Bahá'u'lláh

Nine months before His passing Bahá'u'lláh had, according to 'Abdu'l-Bahá, 'voiced His desire to depart from this world'. On 8 May 1892, He manifested an apparently slight illness with fever which, after a brief remission, recurred and became alarming.

Six days before He passed away He summoned to His presence . . . the entire company of believers, including several pilgrims, . . . for what proved to be their last audience with Him. 'I am well pleased with you all,' He gently and affectionately addressed the weeping crowd that gathered about Him. 'Ye have rendered many services, and been very assiduous in your labours. Ye have come here every morning and every evening. May God assist you to remain united. May He aid you to exalt the Cause of the Lord of being.' (*God Passes By*, p. 222)

He continued to grant interviews to certain of the friends and pilgrims, but it soon became evident that He was not well. His fever returned in a more acute form than before,[5] His general condition grew steadily worse, complications ensued which at last culminated in His ascension, at the hour of dawn, on the 2nd of Dhi'l-Qa'dih 1309 AH (29 May 1892), eight hours after sunset, in the 75th year of His age. His spirit, at long last released from the toils of a life crowded with tribulations, had winged its flight to His 'other dominions', dominions 'whereon the eyes of the people of names have never fallen', and to which the 'Luminous Maid', 'clad in white', had bidden Him hasten, as described by Himself in the *Lawḥ-i-Ru'yá* (Tablet of the Vision), revealed nineteen years previously, on the anniversary of the birth of His Forerunner. (ibid. p. 221)

The news of His ascension was instantly communicated to Sulṭán 'Abdu'l-Ḥamíd in a telegram which began with the words 'the Sun of Bahá has set' and in which the monarch was advised of the intention of interring the sacred remains within the precincts of the Mansion, an arrangement to which he readily assented. Bahá'u'lláh was accordingly laid to rest in the northernmost room of the house which served as a dwelling-place for His son-in-law,[6] the most northerly of the three houses lying to the west of, and adjacent to, the Mansion. His interment took place shortly after sunset, on the very day of His ascension.[7] (ibid. p. 222)

On that day of the ascension of Bahá'u'lláh to the heavenly realms, the room wherein His Holy Dust was laid became the centre of pilgrimage, the Shrine of Shrines, the Most Holy Spot, the Qiblih of the Bahá'í world for at least the next thousand years. Of the wonder of Bahá'u'lláh's achievements as a prisoner and an exile, 'Abdu'l-Bahá has written:

'His enemies intended that His imprisonment should completely destroy and annihilate the blessed Cause, but this prison was, in reality, of the greatest assistance, and became the means of its development.' '. . .This illustrious Being uplifted His Cause in the Most Great Prison. From this Prison His light was shed abroad; His fame conquered the world, and the proclamation of His glory reached the East and the West.' 'His light at first had been a star; now it became a mighty sun.' 'Until our time, no such thing has ever occurred.' (ibid. p. 196)

The Shrine of Bahá'u'lláh from the north. Steady development of the gardens surrounding the Shrine had begun, and a first simple entrance existed.

112

19 Bahjí: Days of Sorrow and Regeneration

ON THE NINTH DAY after the Blessed Beauty's passing. His Will and Testament, the *Kitáb-i-'Ahd*, which He had entrusted to 'Abdu'l-Bahá, was brought from 'Akká to Bahjí at the Master's order, and was unsealed before nine witnesses. It was subsequently read 'on the afternoon of that same day, before a large company assembled in His Most Holy Tomb', after which 'Abdu'l-Bahá returned to 'Akká, despite the fact that a cholera epidemic had broken out, exciting most of the inhabitants to flee in panic. After a further nine days, He sent a message to the Bahá'ís throughout the world, calling for steadfastness in the Cause:

The world's great Light, once resplendent upon all mankind, hath set, to shine everlastingly from the Abhá Horizon, His Kingdom of fadeless glory, shedding splendour upon His loved ones from on high and breathing into their hearts and souls the breath of eternal life . . .

O ye beloved of the Lord! Beware, beware lest ye hesitate and waver. Let not fear fall upon you, neither be troubled nor dismayed. Take ye good heed lest this calamitous day slacken the flames of your ardour, and quench your tender hopes. Today is the day for steadfastness and constancy. Blessed are they that stand firm and immovable as the rock and brave the storm and stress of this tempestuous hour. They, verily, shall be the recipients of God's grace; they, verily, shall receive His divine assistance, and shall be truly victorious . . .

The Sun of Truth, that Most Great Light, hath set upon the horizon of the world to rise with deathless splendour over the Realm of the Limitless. In His Most Holy Book He calleth the firm and steadfast of His friends: 'Be not dismayed, O peoples of the world, when the day-star of My beauty is set, and the heaven of My tabernacle is concealed from your eyes. Arise to further My Cause, and to exalt My Word amongst men.' ('Abdu'l-Bahá, *Selections*, pp. 17–18)

Already the first intimations of discontent were being manifested by the Master's half-brother, Muḥammad-'Alí, who refused to deliver the papers of Bahá'u'lláh to Him. Opposition to 'Abdu'l-Bahá, Whose primacy had clearly been established by the Will of Bahá'u'lláh, rapidly increased in intensity; the ambition, jealousy and misrepresentations of Muḥammad-'Alí culminated in the open disaffection of his family and a number of others.

Forsaken, betrayed, assaulted by almost the entire body of His relatives, now congregated in the Mansion and the neighbouring houses clustering around the most Holy Tomb, 'Abdu'l-Bahá, already bereft of both His mother and His sons, and without any support at all save that of an unmarried sister, His four unmarried daughters, His wife and His uncle (a half-brother of Bahá'u'lláh), was left alone to bear, in the face of a multitude of enemies arrayed against Him from within and from without, the full brunt of the terrific responsibilities which His exalted office had laid upon Him. (*God Passes By*, p. 247)

Unfortunately for the splendid Mansion and its supernal associations and experiences, Covenant-breaker families occupied it and the houses in the immediate vicinity for long decades. Yet during the whole of His remaining years the Master continued to bring the faithful pilgrims to the Shrine, shielding them from the virulent attacks often made upon them in 'Akká or at Bahjí. He had possession of the Tea House[1] at the southern edge of the property and had rented the house now known as the Pilgrim House.[2] Boldly He took the pil-

The Pilgrim House at Bahjí and its western doorway (Baker, early 1930s)

The Tea House at the southern edge of Bahjí, with buildings of the Baydún estate behind. Note the roof-top room and shelters, and the arbours built at the enclosing wall.

'Abdu'l-Bahá on His white
donkey at the western door
of the Pilgrim House, Bahjí
(c. 1920)

grims to the Holiest Shrine even when Covenant-breakers
occupied that very house wherein the Shrine was located, for
such visitation was their inalienable right.

Over the years a slow and terrible decay fell upon the glorious property from which had emanated such spiritual power,
until its appearance seemed to reflect the corrupt personalities
housed there. With the passing of 'Abdu'l-Bahá in 1921 and the
beginning of the ministry of Shoghi Effendi, a further wave of
malevolence was aimed at the emerging World Centre, which
was accompanied by additional physical decay of the properties.

As the beloved Guardian steadfastly pursued his responsibilities in the 1920s, he was enveloped in a miasma of duplicity
and virulent assault upon himself and the developing institutions of the Faith. Muḥammad-'Alí was unregenerate, as were
his brothers and many of his associates. But persistently and

115

The Mansion of Bahjí at the time when the Guardian regained its custody and began its restoration from its sad state of neglect (1929)

Western gallery of the Mansion before the beginning of restoration (1929)

resolutely Shoghi Effendi invoked justice from the new British Mandate authorities in the matter of property ownership.

First he gained the formal right of access to the Tomb of Bahá'u'lláh through the Covenant-breakers' own actions:

The Covenant-breakers, now dwindled to a mere handful, instigated by Mírzá Muḥammad-'Alí, the Arch-rebel, whose dormant hopes had been awakened by 'Abdu'l-Bahá's sudden ascension, and headed by the arrogant Mírzá Badí'u'lláh, seized forcibly the keys of the Tomb of Bahá'u'lláh, expelled its keeper, the brave-souled Abu'l-Qásim-i-Khurásání, and demanded that their chief be recognized by the authorities as the legal custodian of that Shrine. (ibid. p. 355)

The main hall of the Mansion just before the Guardian began its restoration (1929)

This seizure was reversed by 'firm action of the Palestine authorities, who, after prolonged investigations, instructed the British officer in 'Akká to deliver the keys into the hands of that same keeper. . .' (ibid.)

Next, in 1929 Shoghi Effendi gained legal recognition of the Faith as an independent religious community with 'full powers to administer its own affairs now enjoyed by other religious communities in Palestine'. The keys for the Mansion of Bahjí were placed in his hands and he immediately began the process of restoration.

The divine justice working inexorably upon Muḥammad-'Alí and his accomplices throughout those sad years is described by Shoghi Effendi:

116

As to those who had openly espoused the cause of this arch-breaker of Bahá'u'lláh's Covenant, or who had secretly sympathized with him, whilst outwardly supporting 'Abdu'l-Bahá, some eventually repented and were forgiven; others became disillusioned and lost their faith entirely; a few apostatized, whilst the rest dwindled away, leaving him in the end, except for a handful of his relatives, alone and unsupported. Surviving 'Abdu'l-Bahá by almost twenty years, he who had so audaciously affirmed to His face that he had no assurance he might outlive Him, lived long enough to witness the utter bankruptcy of his cause, leading meanwhile a wretched existence within the walls of a Mansion that had once housed a crowd of his supporters; was denied by the civil authorities, as a result of the crisis he had after 'Abdu'l-Bahá's passing foolishly precipitated, the official custody of his Father's Tomb; was compelled, a few years later, to vacate that same Mansion, which, through his flagrant neglect, had fallen into a dilapidated condition; was stricken with paralysis which crippled half his body; lay bedridden in pain for months before he died;[3] and was buried according to Muslim rites, in the immediate vicinity of a local Muslim shrine, his grave remaining until the present day devoid of even a tombstone – a pitiful reminder of the

pilgrim's first view of the Mansion when approaching from the south along the wall of the Baydún estate. The mountains on the Lebanon border (the Ladder of Tyre) are seen in the background.

The Mansion of Bahjí and surrounding buildings: at the far left the Pilgrim House (1), and the building removed soon thereafter (2), Covenant-breaker apartment house on the north removed in 1958 (3), houses at the east wall of the Mansion removed in the 1950s (4), and the room of Údí Khammár's tomb (5). (c. 1930s)

117

hollowness of the claims he had advanced, of the depths of infamy to which he had sunk, and of the severity of the retribution his acts had so richly merited. (ibid. p. 320)

Long years later, with the establishment of the State of Israel by the United Nations in 1947 and during the 1948 war which followed, many Covenant-breakers fled the country, relieving the Guardian of their noxious presence. In 1952 an extensive acreage, including the houses in the immediate vicinity of the Mansion,[4] was exchanged by the Government of Israel for the Ein Gev properties given to Shoghi Effendi by the family of Mírzá Muḥammad-Qulí, loyal half-brother of Bahá'u'lláh and companion of His exile. In that year Shoghi Effendi twice cabled the Bahá'í world to tell of this great achievement and of the steps immediately undertaken.

SIGNAL SUCCESS REMOVAL RUINS IMMEDIATELY FOLLOWED LANDSCAPING APPROACHES SHRINE ERECTION GATE EMBELLISH-MENT SURROUNDINGS TOMB BAHÁ'U'LLÁH . . . (11 June 1952)

In his second cablegram the Guardian related the events

Aerial view of Bahjí during the early development by the Guardian of the north-western quadrant, the Ḥaram-i-Aqdas (Most Holy Precincts). Note that the hill has not yet been raised, nor the northern apartment house demolished to cleanse the property.

...erial view showing the ...mplex of buildings at ...hjí. At the left (west) are ...ree houses in a row, the ...permost being the Shrine ...Bahá'u'lláh, the lowest ...e pilgrim house, the ...ntre house now gutted ...ve for external walls. The ...ansion of Bahjí, as ...stored by Shoghi Effendi, ...d his development of the ...rdens are well seen. The ...ovenant-breaker houses ...the north and east are ...on to be eliminated. ...954)

which made possible the safeguarding of the Tomb and the Mansion, and joyfully projected his plans:

ANNOUNCE BAHÁ'Í COMMUNITIES EAST WEST . . . COMMENCE-MENT LARGE SCALE LANDSCAPING AIMING BEAUTIFICATION IMMEDIATE PRECINCTS HOLIEST SPOT ENTIRE BAHÁ'Í WORLD ITSELF PRELUDE EVENTUAL ERECTION . . . BEFITTING MAUSO-LEUM ENSHRINING PRECIOUS DUST MOST GREAT NAME. (12 November 1952)

Finally, he reported in his 1957 Convention message the eviction order against the Covenant-breakers, 'which, when carried out, will mark the final cleansing, after more than sixty-five years, of the immediate surroundings of the holiest Spot in the Bahá'í world'.

The great steps of triumphant rehabilitation of the Mansion have been summarized by Shoghi Effendi:

The evacuation of the Mansion of Bahá'u'lláh by these Covenant-breakers, after their unchallenged occupancy of it since His ascension, a Mansion which, through their gross neglect, had fallen into a sad state of disrepair; its subsequent complete restoration, fulfilling a long cherished desire of 'Abdu'l-Bahá; its illumination through an electric plant installed by an American believer [Curtis Kelsey] for that purpose; the refurnishing of all its rooms after it had been completely denuded by its former occupants of all the precious relics it contained, with the exception of a single candlestick in the room where Bahá'u'lláh had ascended; the collection within its walls of Bahá'í historic documents, of relics and of over five thousand volumes of Bahá'í literature, in no less than forty languages; the extension to it of the exemption from government taxes, already granted to other Bahá'í institutions and properties in 'Akká and on Mt. Carmel; and finally, its conversion from a private residence to a centre of pilgrimage visited by Bahá'ís and non–Bahá'ís alike – these served to further dash the hopes of those who were still desperately striving to extinguish the light of the Covenant of Bahá'u'lláh. (*God Passes By*, p. 356)

Mansion of Bahá'u'lláh, southern face, with gateway into its courtyard. A company of pilgrims and local Bahá'ís approach the Holy Places. Note the doorway on the far right which opens into the tomb of 'Údí Khammár.

Later Years of Development

In the midst of his struggles to regain the holy properties the beloved Guardian set out to realize his grand goals for Bahjí.

120

The Shrine building and Pilgrim House were restored to beauty and serenity. Great enveloping gardens were conceived as a befitting setting for the Jewel which was the Shrine, and for the Mansion where Revelation had seen its fulfilment and which had witnessed the passing of God's Manifestation. The development of the Shrine in its setting was a task which would necessarily involve many decades of work, even into the next century, but the Guardian initiated the process with characteristic ardour, and with the loving support of the believers world-wide.

Shrine of Bahá'u'lláh, northern face, showing the new portico following its installation

The great surrounding park, with the Shrine and Mansion at its centre, emerged in the form of a huge cross with the two primary buildings at the centre square, its angles filled by the four quadrants of an exploded circle, each quadrant becoming a garden of different composition and quality. Beginning with the most important garden, that which focused upon the Shrine, the Guardian supervised the creation of the Ḥaram-i-Aqdas, the Most Holy Precincts. Often he spent nights in the Mansion and then, from his little blockhouse north-west of the Mansion near the pine grove, acted as overseer of the vital

121

work. The grove of pines has not survived save for the two trees which lay outside the perimeter of the quadrant, and he spared the old sycamore fig tree growing in what came to be a principal pathway. He built the five gates and nine pathways of the Ḥaram-i-Aqdas, surfacing most of the paths with crushed roof tiles, some of which came from the demolition of houses once occupied by Covenant-breakers. The main path he covered with small white pebbles from a beach on the Sea of Galilee. He purchased abroad the monuments which lined the main avenue to the Shrine and which edged the paths of the outer circle. He supervised the choice of plants and their plantings. He built a befitting portico for the Shrine and in 1957 replaced the original door for that holy Place with a more beautiful one. He erected the splendid wrought-iron gate at the northern approach, naming it after the Hand of the Cause Amelia Collins. And he was far advanced in this vital development of the Shrine setting when, in November 1957, he was tragically stricken in London.

The Hands of the Cause, during the following six years, completed certain of the work begun, including the final removal of all the houses and accessory buildings surrounding the Shrine and Mansion, thus fulfilling the 'cleansing' which Shoghi Effendi had ordered. With the rubbish of that demolition the northern hillock with its terraces was completed and became a vantage point for viewing the Shrine, the Mansion and the Ḥaram-i-Aqdas.

It remained for the Universal House of Justice from 1963 onwards to carry still further the grand plan of the Guardian: first the development of the north-eastern quadrant, then the south-eastern quadrant and finally the south-western one, each with different patterns, plants and designs, preserving meanwhile the extensive olive grove of the south and west. A bequest of property from a loyal adherent in 'Akká as an international endowment made possible the acquisition by exchange of an important tract at Bahjí's southern gateway adjacent to the Baydún property. The western gateway was fashioned and gave ready access to the property from the Nahariya road. The northern approaches have been designed and are being developed to the central gardens from Shomrat Road, where in time the main access gate will be constructed. Acquisition in September 1980 of additional land in the south-western area has permitted completion of the fourth quadrant of the gardens surrounding the Most Holy Shrine.

View eastward to the hills of the western Galilee where are located (here unseen) the Druze villages of Yerka and Jatt. In midground left the village of Shaykh Dawúd (David) and at right the village of Shaykh Dannún (Thulnoon in Bahá'í notes). (Getsinger c. 1900)

20 Other Sites Related to the Faith in the Environs of 'Akká

THE LATTER YEARS of Bahá'u'lláh's life, when He had been released from the confinement of the prison city, were marked by a series of local journeys taken in the vicinity of 'Akká.

On 18 or 19 June 1880, just following the return of 'Abdu'l-Bahá from Beirut, Bahá'u'lláh set forth for a visit to the Druze village of Yirkih (Yerka), where He remained for seven nights. 'Abdu'l-Bahá came to the village for the last four nights of that sojourn; another record tells of His stay in that same village for some three months. Small wonder that His room is held to this day as a place of veneration there. He also visited the Druze village of Abú-Sinán, and passed through or close to the hamlets of Ghabsíyyih, Shaykh Dannún (Thulnoon), and Shaykh Dawúd along the valley of the north Asherat brook to the garden of Ḥumaymih near the third spring of Kabrí and the village of An-Nahr. The garden at that time was owned by Muḥammad al-'Afífí, the Persian consul in 'Akká, and was a place of rustic delight, of running water and shady arbours, warm with the hospitality of an admiring host. It is recorded that He pitched His tent on the adjacent tell Naḥaf, where once successive ancient villages had stood.

Several of the Bahá'ís acquired a property north-west of Mazra'ih in the outskirts of Nahariya, a garden called the Junaynih, which in 1901 was registered under the names of 'Abdu'l-Bahá and a brother; adjacent lots were owned by the Jarráh family. Edward Granville Browne mentions seeing the Blessed Beauty at the garden during his 1890 visit. It was a site favoured and often visited by Bahá'u'lláh.

Just above Bahjí, on the road to Nahariya, was a hillock which in the rainy season was singularly brilliant with wild flowers, a place where, as the spring weeks passed, red blooms presented bright displays: crown anemones, then Sharon tulips, turban buttercups,[1] adonis, and lastly true poppies as climax. Named Samaríyyih Hill, Bahá'u'lláh termed it 'the Crimson Hill' (*Buq'atu'l-Ḥamrá'*) in His Writings, mirroring His joy at God's beauty in nature. He had his tent pitched there on occasion. Presently the hill is occupied by a small military camp situated opposite the Kibbutz and Museum of the Ghetto Fighters of Warsaw (Loḥamei Hagetaot).

Twice He pitched His tent near the tell of ancient Acco-Ptolemais just north of the Riḍván and Firdaws Gardens.

'Abdu'l-Bahá felt Himself under far less constraint than did Bahá'u'lláh, hence moved about freely, probably touching upon very many sites round about 'Akká. A notable event was the Master's sending the Bahá'ís for asylum to Abú-Sinán in the early months of World War I; during that dangerous period He Himself was frequently in the village, but also maintained His straitened activities in wartime 'Akká and Haifa. He is also known to have visited the Druze of the Carmel, and He owned land in the vicinity of 'Isfiya ('Aṣfiyyih).

Arbours of the Garden of 'Afífí, where Bahá'u'lláh visited the Persian consul, Muḥammad al-'Afífí. Water from a fountain flows beneath the arbour. (Getsinger, *c.* 1900)

21   Water for 'Akká: the Springs and the Aqueduct

The Spring of the Cow and the Spring of the Woman

THE PRESENT CITY of 'Akká lies upon a flat sandstone peninsula essentially bare of soil, at the sea edge, with no natural sources of fresh water existing within its walls; there are only man-made cisterns holding winter rainwater. The nearby muddy Na'mayn River is at tidal level, and brackish for some distance from its mouth, hence is unsatisfactory as a source of fresh water. Outside the present moat, some 300-400 metres to the east, two springs have flowed copiously throughout the centuries, although their combined volume has never been adequate to supply the population of the city. The Spring of the Cow ('Aynu'l-Baqar)[1] once poured forth at a point half-way to the tell of 'Akká, north-east of the walls, and the Spring of the Woman ('Ayn'u-Sitt) lay perhaps 200 metres to the south of it.

In *Epistle to the Son of the Wolf* Bahá'u'lláh quotes passages from Islamic traditions attributed to the Apostle of God Himself:

I bring you tidings of a city betwixt two mountains in Syria, in the middle of a meadow, which is called 'Akká. Verily, he that entereth therein, longing for it and eager to visit it, God will forgive his sins, both of the past and of the future. And he that departeth from it, other than as a pilgrim, God will not bless his departure. In it is a spring called the Spring of the Cow. Whoso drinketh a draught therefrom, God will fill his heart with light, and will protect him from the most great terror on the Day of Resurrection. (p. 178)

Another tradition records:

Blessed the one that hath drunk from the Spring of the Cow and washed in its waters, for the black-eyed damsels quaff the camphor in Paradise, which hath come from the Spring of the Cow, and from

The Druze village of Abú-Sinán on its hill near the Arab town of Kfar Yasíf. A view eastward to the Galilee hills (1972)

125

the Spring of Salván (Siloam), and the Well of Zamzam. Well is it with him that hath drunk from these springs, and washed in their waters, for God hath forbidden the fire of hell to touch him and his body on the Day of Resurrection. (ibid. p. 180)

These incredible passages must have been a puzzle to devout Muslims through the long centuries when 'Akká was only another Arab port on the Mediterranean coast, albeit a strategic and valuable one. Their fulfilment in the Bahá'í Faith is another extraordinary realization of prophecy.

The fame and traditions of past ages concerning the springs have counted for nothing, however, in the face of the water demands of modern Israel. Wells sunk in recent years have intercepted the sub-surface gravels of 'Akká plain, which formerly carried the water from the hills to the springs at the edge of the city. Both springs are now dry, their sites filled in. Not even a monument marks the place of the Spring of the Cow where Adam's mythical ox once watered, a spot presently within the complex of a paint factory. The roadside stonework of the Spring of the Woman, which even recently saw women filling their water-jars from it, was finally destroyed in 1977. Already both springs are fading memories of the time when the thirsty city largely depended upon their bounty.

The Springs of Kabrí and the Aqueduct

The springs close to 'Akká were insufficient for the city's needs in any event, but distant ones were accessible by means of familiar if ancient engineering solutions; remnants of old

The aqueduct of Sulaymán just above Bahjí at Kibbutz Lohamei-Hagetaot. The Crimson Hill mentioned by Bahá'u'lláh, now the site of a small military camp, is seen through the arches.

aqueducts are found around the springs. Thus when, beginning
in 1749, the city was methodically rebuilt from the centuries-
long desolation of Mameluke destruction, Páshá Aḥmad al-
Jazzár constructed an aqueduct to the springs of Kabrí some 13
kilometres to the north-east. But Napoleon's army destroyed
this aqueduct during the siege of 1799, and only traces of it
now remain, its stones having been carried off for other
construction needs.

Sulaymán Páshá, who ruled 'Akká and the district from
1805, in about 1815 undertook to replace the aqueduct, choos-
ing a partially new line northward along the coastal sandstone
ridge to a point just above the hamlet of Mazra'ih (now the
land of Kibbutz Evron), thence by pipe across the valley eastward to the third spring of Kabrí, then apparently by alternat-
ing pipe and aqueduct to connect the second and first springs;
the first spring is located just south of the present Kibbutz
Kabrí. For this work Sulaymán is said to have employed two
Armenian master masons who supervised construction.

The Springs of Kabrí,[2] which supplied the water needed not
only by the city but also by the farmers of the countryside

above 'Akká, are splendid, limestone-fissure springs which spew out water earlier fallen as rain in the Galilee hills. Throughout recent history the abundant year-round water has been the key to important agricultural production, and ruins of ancient villages along the Asherat Valley pay mute testimony to past abundance. The spring mouths were captured and protected by masonry structures which channelled the outflows into the aqueducts or out into the fields. Spring number three, now on the land of Kibbutz Ben-Ami, is close to the site of the small tell Naḥaf of a very old settlement. The little valley adjacent was the site of the Garden of 'Afífí (near the now vanished village of An-Nahr), visited by Bahá'u'lláh at the end of His journey through the Druze villages of Abú-Sinán and Yirkih (Yerka), and through the Arab villages of Shaykh Dannún (Thulnoon) and Shaykh Dawúd.

The aqueduct appears to have been one of the casualties of misrule following the Egyptian occupation of 1831-40, for by the time of the coming of the Great Exile to 'Akká in 1868 it was no longer satisfactorily delivering its precious water. When, however, the 'sagacious and humane governor' Aḥmad Big Tawfíq became Páshá of the city, and when his association with 'Abdu'l-Bahá and perusal of the literature of the Faith had kindled in his heart a new devotion, at an audience with Bahá'u'lláh '. . . the suggestion was made to him to restore the aqueduct which for thirty years had been allowed to fall into disuse – a suggestion which he immediately arose to carry out'. (*God Passes By*, p. 192) One can imagine the joy of the inhabitants at the repair of the aqueduct and the regulation of the precious waters flowing down from Kabrí.

The aqueduct had many vicissitudes in the seventy-five years from Aḥmad Big Tawfíq to the time when, with the coming of the State of Israel, the water of the springs was incorporated into the national water system. Pumps now send the spring waters by pipe to wherever there is need. The old masonry works and aqueduct arches have meanwhile become picturesque monuments to an earlier mode of water transport to the needy city of 'Akká.

Two portions of the aqueduct are of great interest to Bahá'ís: the segment bisecting the Mazra'ih property, and the serpentine segment running longitudinally through Bahjí to the pool of the erstwhile Baydún estate and, beyond, to the pipes and standpipes which finally delivered water to fortress 'Akká.

Holding and diversion basins were constructed at intervals along the course of the aqueduct to permit tapping-off of water for the fields or for domestic use. Two basins lie on or near to the property at the Mansion of Mazra'ih, and another lies buried in the heart of the Ḥaram-i-Aqdas at Bahjí, near the great sycamore fig tree. Both sections traversing the Bahá'í Holy Places are preserved as historic mementoes of settings recalling Bahá'u'lláh's life.

Bahjí from the pine grove. A section of the aqueduct crosses what was to become the Ḥaram-i-Aqdas, behind the sycamore fig tree and in front of the horse-drawn carriage and flock.

Haifa

22 Haifa and Mount Carmel

ACROSS THE BAY from 'Akká the town of Haifa was undergoing a steady growth throughout the nineteenth century, breaking out of the walls constructed in the previous century by Záhiru'l-'Umar, expanding both westward and eastward. As 'Akká's fortunes diminished, Haifa's increased. Communication continued between the two small towns largely through traffic using the beach, bypassing the Kishon and Na'mayn swamps and the dunes, or following the edge of the eastern hills along the old caravan track. In the late 1860s and 1870s a German sect from Württemberg calling itself the Temple Society settled in Israel, with its principal colony on farmland at the foot of Mount Carmel near its western cape. The Christian monastery of the Roman Catholic Carmelite Order, isolated atop Carmel, enjoyed the cooler climate of the high plateau, to reach which the monks later fashioned a well-graded road up the precipitous north face to the holy place of Elijah and its hospice.

To the Prophet Who so loved the rugged mountains of His native Núr in Mázindarán, the spiritual attraction of the Prophet Elijah's Mount Carmel could not but be a strong one. Thus, in 1891

Bahá'u'lláh's tent, the 'Tabernacle of Glory', was raised on Mt. Carmel, 'the Hill of God and His Vineyard', the home of Elijah, extolled by Isaiah as the 'mountain of the Lord', to which 'all nations shall flow'. Four times He visited Haifa, His last visit being no less than three months long. In the course of one of these visits, when His tent was pitched in the vicinity of the Carmelite Monastery, He, the 'Lord of the Vineyard', revealed the *Tablet of Carmel*, remarkable for its allusions and prophecies . . . (*God Passes By*, p. 194)

'Haste thee, O Carmel!' Bahá'u'lláh, significantly addressing that holy mountain, has written, 'for lo, the light of the Countenance of God . . . hath been lifted upon thee . . . Rejoice, for God hath, in this Day, established upon thee His throne, hath made thee the

Aerial photograph showing development of the Shrine gardens, the Pilgrim House, the International Bahá'í Archives, the Monument Gardens and the arc. (1975)

133

dawning-place of His signs and the dayspring of the evidences of His Revelation. Well is it with him that circleth around thee, that proclaimeth the revelation of thy glory, and recounteth that which the bounty of the Lord thy God hath showered upon thee.' 'Call out to Zion, O Carmel!' He, furthermore, has revealed in that same Tablet, 'and announce the joyful tidings: He that was hidden from mortal eyes is come! His all-conquering sovereignty is manifest; His all-encompassing splendour is revealed. Beware lest thou hesitate or halt. Hasten forth and circumambulate the City of God that hath descended from heaven, the celestial Kaaba round which have circled in adoration the favoured of God, the pure in heart, and the company of the most exalted angels.' (ibid. pp. 277–8)

One day in 1891 He ascended the mountain to a group of cypresses above the German Templer colony and partook of afternoon tea. Presumably on that occasion He Himself pointed out to 'Abdu'l-Bahá, as They 'stood on the slopes of that mountain, the site which was to serve as the permanent resting-place of the Báb, and on which a befitting mausoleum was later to be erected'. (*God Passes By*, p. 194) The site where

Bahá'u'lláh stood, with its circle of tall cypresses, is directly behind that Shrine.

Haifa continued to expand, for the German settlers brought a new and strong influence to galvanize Haifa's growth; as one author put it: 'They came to do good, and did extremely well.' Then in 1905 the railroad from Haifa to Damascus and the Ḥijáz was opened. Certainly the British, in deciding in the 1920s to transform Haifa into their principal Middle Eastern naval and oil port, and to build refineries at the terminus of the pipeline from Mosul in 'Iráq, played a decisive role in its development. Haifa was also, for the Zionist Theodor Herzl, the 'city of the future'. But whatever the currents of change and their many causes, 'Abdu'l-Bahá perceived in 1914 what was already surprisingly close, as he visualized it when standing on the balcony of the new Pilgrim House near the Shrine of the Báb (see next chapter), facing the bay and Bahjí beyond:

The view from the Pilgrim House is very attractive, especially as it faces the Blessed Tomb of Bahá'u'lláh. In the future the distance between 'Akká and Haifa will be built up, and the two cities will join and clasp hands, becoming the two terminal sections of one mighty metropolis. As I look now over this scene, I see so clearly that it will become one of the first emporiums of the world. This great semi-circular bay will be transformed into the finest harbour, wherein the ships of all nations will seek shelter and refuge. The great vessels of all peoples will come to this port, bringing on their decks thousands and thousands of men and women from every part of the globe. The mountain and the plain will be dotted with the most modern buildings and palaces. Industries will be established and various institutions of philanthropic nature will be founded. The flowers of civilization and culture from all nations will be brought here to blend their fragrances together and blaze the way for the brotherhood of man. Wonderful gardens, orchards, groves and parks will be laid out on all sides. At night the great city will be lighted by electricity. The entire harbour from 'Akká to Haifa will be one path of illumination. Powerful searchlights will be placed on both sides of Mount Carmel to guide the steamers. Mount Carmel itself, from top to bottom, will be submerged in a sea of lights. A person standing on the summit of Mount Carmel, and the passengers of the steamers coming to it, will look upon the most sublime and majestic spectacle of the whole world.

From every part of the mountain the symphony of 'Yá Bahá'u'l-Abhá' will be raised, and before the daybreak soul-entrancing music accompanied by melodious voices will be uplifted towards the throne of the Almighty. (Esslemont, *Bahá'u'lláh and the New Era*, pp. 252–3)

The clump of cypress trees on the side of Mount Carmel where, in 1891, Bahá'u'lláh indicated to Abdu'l-Bahá the nearby site of the Shrine of the Báb

The Bahá'í Faith has, we believe, provided a powerful if generally unsuspected spiritual stimulus underlying the growth of Haifa. Moreover, the Guardian foreshadowed the great destiny of the Bahá'í properties in the heart of Carmel when he predicted

the splendour of the institutions which that triumphant Faith must erect on the slopes of a mountain, destined to be so linked with the city of 'Akká that a single grand metropolis will be formed to enshrine the spiritual as well as the administrative seats of the future Bahá'í Commonwealth. (*God Passes By*, pp. 315–16)

23   The Shrine of the Báb

FROM THAT DAY in 1891 when Bahá'u'lláh had pointed out the site for the Tomb of His Herald, 'Abdu'l-Bahá had set about realizing the great goal. In 1898 He sent careful and detailed instructions to Mírzá Asadu'lláh-i-Iṣfahání to transport the precious remains of the Blessed Báb from their spot of concealment in Ṭihrán to the Holy Land. This mission Mírzá Asadu'lláh accomplished, with the utmost circumspection and great difficulty, the Holy Dust arriving secretly in 'Akká from Beirut by sea on 31 January 1899.

In the same year that this precious Trust reached the shores of the Holy Land and was delivered into the hands of 'Abdu'l-Bahá, He . . . drove to the recently purchased site which had been blessed and selected by Bahá'u'lláh on Mt. Carmel, and there laid, with His own hands, the foundation-stone of the edifice, the construction of which He, a few months later, was to commence. About that same time, the marble sarcophagus, designed to receive the body of the Báb, an offering of love from the Bahá'ís of Rangoon, had, at 'Abdu'l-Bahá's suggestion, been completed and shipped to Haifa. (*God Passes By*, pp. 274–5)

The construction of a befitting mausoleum on the chosen site

Mount Carmel as seen from its base at present-day Hagefen Street and Ben-Gurion Avenue. Half-way up the mountain, at the clump of cypresses, is the original building of the Shrine of the Báb; at the base of the mountain is the home of the Templer family named Bubeck. (Getsinger, *c.* 1900)

136

was, however, fraught with obstacles.

The long-drawn-out negotiations with the shrewd and calculating owner of the building-site of the holy Edifice, who, under the influence of the Covenant-breakers, refused for a long time to sell; the exorbitant price at first demanded for the opening of a road leading to that site and indispensable to the work of construction; the interminable objections raised by officials, high and low, whose easily aroused suspicions had to be allayed by repeated explanations and assurances given by 'Abdu'l-Bahá Himself; the dangerous situation created by the monstrous accusations brought by Mírzá Muḥammad-'Alí and his associates regarding the character and purpose of that building; the delays and complications caused by 'Abdu'l-Bahá's prolonged and enforced absence from Haifa, and His consequent inability to supervise in person the vast undertaking He had initiated – all these were among the principal obstacles which He, at so critical a period in His ministry, had to face and surmount ere He could execute in its entirety the Plan, the outline of which Bahá'u'lláh had communicated to Him on the occasion of one of His visits to Mt. Carmel.

'Every stone of that building, every stone of the road leading to it,' He, many a time, was heard to remark, 'I have with infinite tears and at tremendous cost, raised and placed in position.' 'One night,' He, according to an eyewitness, once observed, 'I was so hemmed in by My anxieties that I had no other recourse than to recite and repeat over and over again a prayer of the Báb which I had in My possession, the recital of which greatly calmed Me. The next morning the owner of the plot himself came to Me, apologized and begged Me to purchase his property.'

Finally, . . . 'Abdu'l-Bahá brought His undertaking to a successful conclusion, in spite of the incessant machinations of enemies both within and without. On the 28th of the month of Ṣafar 1327 AH, the day of the first Naw-Rúz (1909), which He celebrated after His release from His confinement, 'Abdu'l-Bahá had the marble sarcophagus transported with great labour to the vault prepared for it, and in the evening, by the light of a single lamp, He laid within it, with His own hands – in the presence of believers from the East and from the West and in circumstances at once solemn and moving – the wooden casket containing the sacred remains of the Báb and His companion.

When all was finished, and the earthly remains of the Martyr-Prophet of S͟híráz were, at long last, safely deposited for their everlasting rest in the bosom of God's holy mountain, 'Abdu'l-Bahá, Who had cast aside His turban, removed His shoes and thrown off His cloak, bent low over the still open sarcophagus, His silver hair waving about His head and His face transfigured and luminous, rested His forehead on the border of the wooden casket, and, sobbing aloud, wept with such a weeping that all those who were present wept with Him. That night He could not sleep, so overwhelmed was He with emotion.

'The most joyful tidings is this,' He wrote later in a Tablet announcing to His followers the news of this glorious victory, 'that the holy, the luminous body of the Báb . . . after having for sixty years been transferred from place to place, by reason of the ascendancy of the enemy, and from fear of the malevolent, and having known neither rest nor tranquillity has, through the mercy of the Abhá Beauty, been ceremoniously deposited, on the day of Naw-Rúz, within the sacred casket, in the exalted Shrine on Mt. Carmel . . .'

Shrine of the Báb after cutting of the back wall and completion of the last three rooms

With the transference of the remains of the Báb – Whose advent marks the return of the Prophet Elijah – to Mt. Carmel, and their interment in that holy mountain, not far from the cave of that Prophet Himself, the Plan so gloriously envisaged by Bahá'u'lláh, in the evening of His life, had been at last executed, and the arduous labours associated with the early and tumultuous years of the ministry of the appointed Centre of His Covenant crowned with immortal success. A focal centre of Divine illumination and power, the very dust of which 'Abdu'l-Bahá averred had inspired Him, yielding in sacredness to no other shrine throughout the Bahá'í world except the Sepulchre of the Author of the Bahá'í Revelation Himself, had been permanently established on that mountain, regarded from time immemorial as sacred. A structure, at once massive, simple and imposing; nestling in the heart of Carmel, the 'Vineyard of God'; flanked by the Cave of Elijah on the west, and by the hills of Galilee on the east; backed by the plain of Sharon, and facing the silver-city of 'Akká, and beyond it the Most Holy Tomb, the Heart and Qiblih of the Bahá'í world; overshadowing the colony of German Templars who, in anticipation of the 'coming of the Lord', had forsaken their homes and foregathered at the foot of that mountain, in the very year of Bahá'u'lláh's Declaration in Baghdád (1863), the mausoleum of

139

the Báb had now, with heroic effort and in impregnable strength been established as 'the Spot round which the Concourse on high circle in adoration'. (ibid. pp. 275–7)]

The passing of 'Abdu'l-Bahá in November 1921, and His burial in a northern room of the Shrine, further sanctified that holy edifice which He had brought into existence as one of the paramount objectives of His Mission.

Building of the Superstructure[1]

As the 1940s began, notwithstanding World War II's extension to engulf the nations, the time had come to plan for and build a monumental superstructure, a building which would sheathe the simple square of now nine rooms which contained the precious Dust of the Báb and that of the Master, a building which would fulfil the wishes of the Master. The distinguished Canadian architect William Sutherland Maxwell was at hand in the Guardian's very household, and from him in 1942 Shoghi Effendi requested a design for a befitting edifice. The design was developed step by step in close collaboration with the Guardian, and on 23 May 1944 a model of the superstructure was displayed for the first time, and announced by the Guardian to the Bahá'í world in this message:

. . . Announce friends joyful tidings hundredth anniversary Declaration Mission martyred Herald Faith signalized by historic decision complete structure His Sepulchre erected by 'Abdul'-Bahá site chosen by Bahá'u'lláh. Recently designed model dome unveiled presence assembled believers. Praying early removal obstacles consummation stupendous Plan conceived by Founder Faith and hopes cherished Centre His Covenant. (Rabbani, *The Priceless Pearl*, p. 240)

In April 1946 Shoghi Effendi took active steps to realize this vital goal at the very moment when events in Mandatory Palestine were hurtling towards the outbreak of a new war. In April 1948 contracts were placed in Italy for the rose Baveno granite columns. The work of preparing foundations and the additional cutting of the back wall were initiated, despite the war which was convulsing the new nation of Israel and Haifa itself. In early 1949 construction began and was resolutely

Stages in construction of the Shrine of the Báb: *Above* The building of nine rooms before the addition of the superstructure. *Right* Construction of the colonnade and arcade. *Below left* Completion of the colonnade-arcade at ground level. *Below right* Completion of the octagon.

Stages in construction of the Shrine of the Báb (continued): *Above*
Construction of the drum. *Right and below left* Shaping of the dome.
Below right Completion of the dome and lantern.

prosecuted, whatever the often incredible difficulties within the post-war State of Israel and within an Italy seeking to reconstruct itself after the ravages of World War II. Chiampo marble for the arches, capitals, walls, corners and balustrades was carved in Italy and sent to the Holy Land. Step by step there appeared, as by a miracle, the colonnade and arcade, the octagon, the drum with its 18 lancet windows honouring the Letters of the Living, and finally the crown and dome with its golden tiles and lantern. Sadly, the Hand of the Cause Sutherland Maxwell passed to the Abhá Kingdom in March 1952 without seeing the completion of his final and finest creation. In October 1953, at the New Delhi Intercontinental Teaching Conference commemorating the centenary of the birth of the Mission of Bahá'u'lláh, the Guardian announced the consummation of the noble endeavour begun more than a half-century before, describing the Shrine as the 'QUEEN OF CARMEL ENTHRONED GOD'S MOUNTAIN CROWNED GLOWING GOLD ROBED SHIMMERING WHITE GIRDLED EMERALD GREEN ENCHANTING EVERY EYE FROM AIR SEA PLAIN [and] HILL.' (*The Bahá'í World*, vol. xii, p. 239)

Steadily and with unfaltering energy he pressed forward with the beautification of the gardens which were its emerald

Shrine of the Báb from Ben-Gurion (Carmel) Avenue at the foot of Mount Carmel (1973)

setting, for he saw with clarity the significance of the Shrine, the Holy Dust therein being the focus of a planetary spiritual system:

The outermost circle in this vast system, the visible counterpart of the pivotal position conferred on the Herald of our Faith, is none other than the entire planet. Within the heart of this planet lies the 'Most Holy Land', acclaimed by 'Abdu'l-Bahá as 'the Nest of the Prophets' and which must be regarded as the centre of the world and the Qiblih of the nations. Within this Most Holy Land rises the Mountain of God of immemorial sanctity, the Vineyard of the Lord, the Retreat of Elijah, Whose Return the Báb Himself symbolizes. Reposing on the breast of this Holy Mountain are the extensive properties permanently dedicated to, and constituting the sacred precincts of, the Báb's holy Sepulchre. In the midst of these properties, recognized as the international endowments of the Faith, is situated the Most Holy Court, an enclosure comprising gardens and terraces which at once embellish, and lend a peculiar charm to, these Sacred Precincts. Embosomed in these lovely and verdant surroundings stands in all its exquisite beauty the Mausoleum of the Báb, the Shell designed to preserve and adorn the original structure raised by 'Abdu'l-Bahá as the Tomb of the Martyr-Herald of our Faith. Within this Shell is enshrined that Pearl of Great Price, the Holy of Holies, those chambers which constitute the Tomb itself, and which were constructed by 'Abdu'l-Bahá. Within the heart of this Holy of Holies

Aerial view of the Shrine of the Báb from the north-east, soon after the superstructure had been completed (1954)

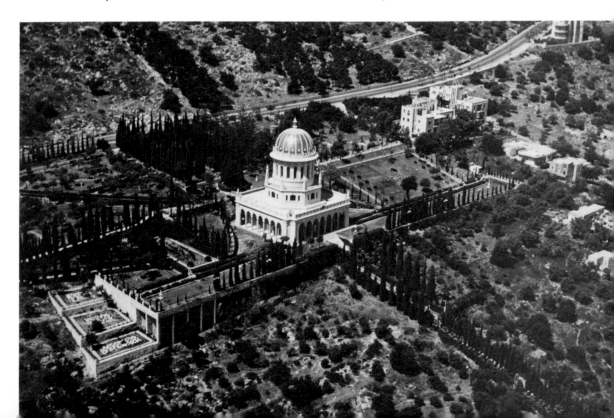

is the Tabernacle, the Vault wherein reposes the Most Holy Casket. Within this Vault rests the alabaster Sarcophagus in which is deposited that inestimable Jewel, the Báb's Holy Dust. So precious is this Dust that the very earth surrounding the Edifice enshrining this Dust has been extolled by the Centre of Bahá'u'lláh's Covenant, in one of His Tablets in which He named the five doors belonging to the six chambers which He originally erected after five of the believers[2] associated with the construction of the Shrine, as being endowed with such potency as to have inspired Him in bestowing these names, whilst the Tomb itself housing this Dust He acclaimed as the Spot round which the Concourse on high circle in adoration. (*The Bahá'í World*, vol. xii, pp. 349–50)

24 The House of the Master

KEENLY AWARE of Bahá'u'lláh's vision of Mount Carmel's great destiny, 'Abdu'l-Bahá, having set Himself to supervise and expedite the erection of the Shrine of the Báb on Mount Carmel, considered building a house in Haifa. Miss Laura Clifford Barney (who became Mme Dreyfus-Barney after her marriage in 1911 to Hippolyte Dreyfus) aided in the purchase of the land at the eastern edge of the German colony, on a lane later to be named Persian (Haparsim) Street. The Master then designed His House, and was assisted by Laura Barney in the construction which followed. Throughout the tense period of the Turkish Commission of Inquiry and in spite of all the malign forces then activated, erection of the House went forward, and its effective completion closely coincided with the rebellion of the Young Turks in 1908. From February 1907 He had begun to transfer the Holy Family to Haifa; in the course of several years all moved from 'Akká, including the Greatest Holy Leaf and His beloved grandson, Shoghi Effendi, and in August 1910 He Himself came to the town across the bay. In this House destined for such great service, and which now became 'Abdu'l-Bahá's official residence, Shoghi Effendi grew to maturity under the Master's tutelage.

In late August 1910 'Abdu'l-Bahá departed from the Holy Land, first to visit Egypt, then proceeding to Europe and North America – travels which were to last more than three years before He returned to Haifa on 5 December 1913, on the eve of the great war whose storm clouds had already brought a bloody rain in the Balkans. Upon His return, the House became the place of reception of pilgrims, and the place of many significant events in Bahá'í history.

During this period of journeys and travail, of conquest of hearts in East and West, the Master was the very image of the seer and sage. As Lady Blomfield described him in 1912:

He wore a low-crowned *táj*, round which was folded a small, fine-linen turban of purest white; His hair and short beard were of that snowy whiteness which had once been black; His eyes were large, blue-grey with long, black lashes and well-marked eyebrows; His face was a beautiful oval with warm, ivory-coloured skin, a straight, finely-modelled nose, and firm, kind mouth . . . His figure was of such perfect symmetry, and so full of dignity and grace, that the first impression was that of considerable height . . . inner grace shone in every glance, and word, and movement as He came with hands outstretched. (*The Bahá'í World*, vol. xiii, p. 1186)

When in October 1914 Turkey entered the First World War on the side of the Central Powers, Britain confronted it in Egypt and 'Iráq. In Palestine fears of Turkish elimination of minorities impelled the Master to remove the Bahá'ís of Haifa and 'Akká to the Druze village of Abú-Sinán, while He Himself stayed much of the time in 'Akká. In May 1915 all returned to their homes, and during the latter half of that year the

147

Master gave biographical talks on early Bahá'ís which were assembled to become the book entitled *Memorials of the Faithful*. During early 1917 He revealed three Tablets of the Divine Plan in the room of 'Ismá'íl Áqá at the edge of the garden of the House in Haifa. On one occasion He visited Nazareth to meet the Turkish General, Jamál Páshá, seeking to ameliorate his hostility towards the Bahá'ís. In the last months of the War, a time of hardship and deprivations, He arranged to feed many of the hungry of the twin cities with grain, much of which was produced and stored by Bahá'í farmers living near the Sea of Galilee. Finally, on 23 September 1918 the British army took Haifa and 'Abdu'l-Bahá was safe from the threat of execution by the Turks.

At the War's ending, Shoghi Effendi, having completed his course of arts and sciences at the American University of Beirut, became 'Abdu'l-Bahá's secretary and translated many of His Tablets to the Bahá'ís of the West. It is touching to recall that during his student holidays, his room being next to 'Abdu'l-Bahá's, the Master many times went to Shoghi Effendi's room at midnight and urged him to stop writing and go to his rest. The fourteen Tablets of the Divine Plan were presented at the American National Convention of 1919, the first five Tablets already having been published in *Star of the West*.

Pilgrims once again began to come to the Centre of their Faith, the first two from the West being Hippolyte and Laura Dreyfus-Barney. Later the House was prepared for the renewed flow of pilgrims. In addition, 'Abdu'l-Bahá built a small structure at the south-western end of the garden which

surrounded the House, and '. . . had the inner walls, the ceiling and floor of one of its upper rooms covered with wood, as a protection against humidity. It was in this room that He slept at nights during the period immediately before His passing.'[1] From this House, in the War's aftermath, 'Abdu'l-Bahá sent His famous Tablet to the Hague. And here He received a

The northern face of the House of 'Abdu'l-Bahá at No. 7 Haparsim Street (Ḥakím, 1920)

The small rooms at the south-western corner of the garden. The room at the left was used by 'Abdu'l-Bahá. (. 1920)

multitude of visitors, ordinary, distinguished and to-become-distinguished, including Dr John Esslemont, General Allenby, Sir Herbert Samuel, and the deposed King Faisal of Syria who later became King of 'Iráq.

On 27 April 1920, a Knighthood of the British Empire was conferred on 'Abdu'l-Bahá in Haifa for His humanitarian service during the War; He accepted the honour as a gift from a 'just king'. On that same day in Wilmette, during the American Convention, the design of Louis Bourgeois was accepted, with 'Abdu'l-Bahá's approval, for the Mother Temple of the Faith in the West. Some time in the spring of 1920 Shoghi Effendi left Haifa for France and England, to continue his studies at Oxford University from October 1920, entering Balliol College in January 1921.

149

The Passing of 'Abdu'l-Bahá

As the Master passed into his seventy-sixth year His ceaseless labours continued, but He Himself was aware that His earthly time was drawing near its close.

His good and faithful servant, Ismá'íl Áqá, relates the following:
'Some time, about twenty days before my Master passed away, I was near the garden when I heard Him summon an old believer saying:
' "Come with me that we may admire together the beauty of the garden. Behold, what the spirit of devotion is able to achieve! This flourishing place was, a few years ago, but a heap of stones, and now it is verdant with foliage and flowers. My desire is that after I am gone the loved ones may all arise to serve the divine cause and, please God, so it shall be. Ere long men will arise who shall bring life to the world". . .'

The Master at the doorway of His House in Haifa (c. 192

In the morning of Saturday, 26 November, He arose early, came to the tea-room, and had some tea. He asked for the fur-lined coat which had belonged to Bahá'u'lláh. He often put on this coat when He was cold or did not feel well, He so loved it. He then withdrew to His room, lay down on His bed, and said, 'Cover me up. I am very cold. Last night I did not sleep well, I felt cold. This is serious, it is the beginning.'

150

After more blankets had been put on, He asked for the fur coat He had taken off to be placed over Him. That day He was rather feverish. In the evening His temperature rose still higher, but during the night the fever left Him. After midnight He asked for some tea.

On Sunday morning, 27 November, He said, 'I am quite well and will get up as usual and have tea with you in the tea-room.' After He had dressed, He was persuaded to remain on the sofa in His room.

In the afternoon He sent all the friends to the tomb of the Báb, where on the occasion of the anniversary of the declaration of the Covenant a feast was being held, offered by a Pársí pilgrim who had lately arrived from India.

At four in the afternoon, being on the sofa in His room, He said, 'Ask my sister and all the family to come and have tea with me.'

His four sons-in-law and Rúḥí Effendi came to Him after returning from the gathering on the mountain. They said to Him, 'The giver of the feast was unhappy because You were not there.' He said unto them:

'But I was there, though my body was absent, my spirit was there in your midst. I was present with the friends at the tomb. The friends must not attach any importance to the absence of my body. In spirit I am, and shall always be, with the friends, even though I be far away.'

The same evening He asked after the health of every member of the household, of the pilgrims, and of the friends in Haifa. 'Very good, very good,' He said when told that none were ill. This was His very last utterance concerning His friends.

At eight in the evening He retired to bed after taking a little nourishment, saying, 'I am quite well.'

He told all the family to go to bed and rest. Two of His daughters, however, stayed with Him. That night the Master had gone to sleep very calmly, quite free from fever. He awoke about 1.15 a.m., got up, and walked across to a table where He drank some water. He took off an outer night garment, saying, 'I am too warm.' He went back to bed; and, when His daughter Rúḥá Khánum, later on, approached, she found Him lying peacefully; and, as He looked into her face, He asked her to lift up the net curtains, saying:

'I have difficulty in breathing, give me more air.' Some rose water was brought of which He drank, sitting up in bed to do so, without any help. He again lay down, and as some food was offered Him, He remarked in a clear and distinct voice:

'You wish me to take some food, and I am going?' He gave them a beautiful look. His face was so calm, His expression so serene, they thought Him asleep.

He had gone from the gaze of His loved ones! (*The Bahá'í World* vol. xv, pp. 114–15)[2]

The room where the Master's ascension to the Abhá Kingdom occurred is on the right as one enters the House. From this

House the cortège left for the Shrine where His blessed remains were interred.

Later Years

During the days of the Guardianship the House was the centre of activities, a place of pilgrimage and the seat of Shoghi Effendi's indefatigable labours in establishing the Faith throughout the world. During his ministry the Guardian continued the Master's practice of receiving guests in the room at the left of the entrance. In the early 1920s an apartment was constructed on the roof to serve as Shoghi Effendi's quarters, and this was expanded in 1937 upon his marriage to Amatu'l-Bahá Rúḥíyyih <u>Kh</u>ánum. In recent years the reception room directly opposite the entrance doorway has been used by Rúḥíyyih <u>Kh</u>ánum to receive pilgrims and guests.

25 The Shrine of 'Abdu'l-Bahá

THE MASTER passed to the Abhá Kingdom in the early morning hours of Monday, 28 November 1921. The news of this sudden calamity rapidly 'spread over the city, causing an unprecedented stir and tumult, and filling all hearts with unutterable grief.' (*The Bahá'í World, supra*)

As to the funeral itself, which took place on Tuesday morning – a funeral the like of which Palestine had never seen – no less than ten thousand people participated representing every class, religion and race in that country . . .

The coffin containing the remains of 'Abdu'l-Bahá was borne to its last resting-place on the shoulders of His loved ones . . .

Close to the eastern entrance of the Shrine, the sacred casket was placed upon a plain table, and, in the presence of that vast concourse, nine speakers, who represented the Muslim, the Jewish and Christian Faiths, and who included the Muftí of Haifa, delivered their several funeral orations. These concluded, the High Commissioner drew

close to the casket, and, with bowed head fronting the Shrine, paid his last homage of farewell to 'Abdu'l-Bahá: the other officials of the Government followed his example. The coffin was then removed to one of the chambers of the Shrine, and there lowered, sadly and reverently, to its last resting-place in a vault adjoining that in which were laid the remains of the Báb. (*God Passes By*, pp. 312–13)

The three rooms on the north side of the Shrine of the Báb comprise the central room where the remains of the Master are buried, the western and eastern antechambers serving as places of prayer and visitation for pilgrims, places redolent with the fragrances of the Master's pure spirit, until the time when His precious remains will have found their own Shrine, thus 'enhancing still further the sacredness' of Mount Carmel.

The entrance to the House of the Master, showing the apartment added on the roof by the Guardian (1974)

26   The Axis of the Shrine of the Báb

WITH THE ESTABLISHMENT of the Shrine on Mount Carmel the great plan conceived by 'Abdu'l-Bahá for the present and future Bahá'í properties on the holy mountain was set afoot. One primary goal was to develop the axis of the Shrine from the foot of the mountain to its very top, literally as an extension of Carmel Avenue (now Ben-Gurion Avenue), that wide boulevard which was the main street of the Templer colony and which led from the base of the mountain to the sea, pointing across the bay to 'Akká and Bahjí. The plan called for nine terraces with stairways from the foot of the mountain to the Shrine, and nine above the Shrine to the mountain-top, with the Shrine area constituting the nineteenth terrace.

It fell to Shoghi Effendi to begin this great task of artistry and arduous labour, developing and landscaping the Shrine area itself even as he pursued the difficult acquisition of the additional property on the steep mountainside needed to realize the plan's great scope. Undertaking this aspect of his multitudinous responsibilities with great verve, he demolished the house which lay on the access pathway to the Shrine from the Pilgrim House and in that spot boldly hewed out a new terrace to make possible what is now a splendid rose garden. After cutting away the rock wall behind the Shrine in a handsome arc, he was able, through the munificence of Hájí Mahmúd Qassábchí, to add three additional rooms to the Shrine, thus producing a square building of nine chambers, which completed ''Abdu'l-Bahá's plan for the first unit of that Edifice', the centre room holding beneath its floor the Sacred Dust of the Báb. The three new rooms he devoted to the display of precious Bahá'í relics, thus creating the first international Bahá'í Archives.

Eastward and westward the Guardian extended the great terrace on which stood the Shrine, and erected high retaining walls along the northern and eastern faces. He constructed a splendid stairway downwards from the Shrine to the path which ultimately would become that kingsway up which monarchs of the future would come as pilgrims. Half-way down the path he threw a bridge across the road which transected the property, the road named Abbas Street after the Master. At the bottom of the path he planned a fine gateway, but, never able to resolve obstacles created by the authorities, he erected instead a dignified but temporary access gate. With incessant labour he designed, laid out and built the gardens all about the Shrine until their growing beauty made them a place of visitation for the citizens of Haifa and for a great and growing stream of visitors from around the world. In a few words he summarized this 'vast extension . . . of the properties surrounding that resting-place, sweeping from the ridge of Carmel down to the Templar colony nestling at its foot':

. . . the opening of a series of terraces which, as designed by 'Abdu'l-Bahá, are to provide a direct approach to the Báb's Tomb from the city lying under its shadow; the beautification of its precincts through the laying out of parks and gardens, open daily to the public, and attracting tourists and residents alike to its gates – these may be regarded as the initial evidences of the marvellous expansion of the international institutions and endowments of the Faith at its world centre. (*God Passes By*, p. 346)

27 The Monument Gardens

BAHÁ'U'LLÁH'S VISION of 'the seat of [God's] throne' on Mount Carmel, of a great Bahá'í administrative centre-to-be, early occupied an important part of the Guardian's thoughts and energies as he moved step by step to acquire the additional land needed for his evolving plan and to begin the necessary initial construction on Carmel's stony slopes.

A winding road led up the mountain from the German colony and the port area to the top of Carmel, bisecting the Bahá'í properties and passing above the Shrine through the olive-grove planted where the Shrine now stands. The house at the eastern edge of the upper land-holding became the second International Archives when the accumulating precious relics of the Faith were too many to be properly displayed in the three back rooms of the Shrine. Immediately adjacent to and west of that house Shoghi Effendi began to shape the mountain into a unique garden spot befitting the base of the future arc, where the buildings of the World Administrative Centre would be reared. Later, he made reference to 'the selection of a portion of the school property situated in the precincts of the Shrine of the Báb as a permanent resting-place for the Greatest Holy Leaf . . .' (*God Passes By*, p. 347)

The Greatest Holy Leaf: Bahíyyih <u>Kh</u>ánum

In mid-July 1932 the Guardian's best support was taken away: the Greatest Holy Leaf passed to the Abhá Kingdom. His sorrow leapt from the impassioned cablegram sent to the Bahá'í world on the 15th of that month:

GREATEST HOLY LEAF'S IMMORTAL SPIRIT WINGED ITS FLIGHT GREAT BEYOND STOP COUNTLESS LOVERS HER SAINTLY LIFE IN EAST AND WEST SEIZED WITH PANGS OF ANGUISH PLUNGED UNUTTERABLE SORROW HUMANITY SHALL ERELONG RECOGNIZE ITS IRREPARABLE LOSS STOP OUR BELOVED FAITH WELL NIGH CRUSHED BY DEVASTATING BLOW OF 'ABDU'L-BAHÁ'S UNEX-PECTED ASCENSION NOW LAMENTS PASSING LAST REMNANT OF BAHÁ'U'LLÁH ITS MOST EXALTED MEMBER STOP HOLY FAMILY CRUELLY DIVESTED ITS MOST PRECIOUS GREAT ADORNING STOP I FOR MY PART BEWAIL SUDDEN REMOVAL MY SOLE EARTHLY SUS-TAINER THE JOY AND SOLACE OF MY LIFE STOP REMAINS WILL REPOSE VICINITY HOLY SHRINES STOP SO GRIEVOUS A BEREAVE-MENT NECESSITATES SUSPENSION FOR NINE MONTHS THROUGH-OUT BAHÁ'Í WORLD EVERY MANNER RELIGIOUS FESTIVITY STOP INFORM LOCAL ASSEMBLIES AND GROUPS HOLD BEFITTING MAN-NER MEMORIAL GATHERINGS EXTOL A LIFE SO LADEN SACRED EXPERIENCES SO RICH IMPERISHABLE MEMORIES STOP ADVISE HOLDING ADDITIONAL COMMEMORATION SERVICE OF STRICTLY DEVOTIONAL CHARACTER AUDITORIUM MA<u>SH</u>RIQU'L-A<u>DH</u>KÁR.

When the news of Bahíyyih <u>Kh</u>ánum's passing reached him in Switzerland, Shoghi Effendi's first action was to plan a worthy memorial for her grave, and he then hurried to Italy to commission it.

Two days after her passing he had poured out, from the depths of his grief-stricken heart, his marvellous, immortal tribute to her whom he described as the 'treasured Remnant of

Bahá'u'lláh entrusted to our frail and unworthy hands by our departed Master . . .' Frequently, in the succeeding years he referred in touching eulogies to his beloved great-aunt who had so sustained him throughout his years of lonely tribulation, beset as he was by the enemies of the Faith and consumed with the work of development of the Cause.

It would take me too long to make even a brief allusion to those incidents of her life, each of which eloquently proclaims her as a daughter, worthy to inherit that priceless heritage bequeathed to her by Bahá'u'lláh. A purity of life that reflected itself in even the minutest details of her daily occupations and activities; a tenderness of heart that obliterated every distinction of creed, class and colour; a resignation and serenity that evoked to the mind the calm and heroic fortitude of the Báb; a natural fondness of flowers and children that was so characteristic of Bahá'u'lláh; an unaffected simplicity of manners; an extreme sociability which made her accessible to all; a generosity, a love, at once disinterested and undiscriminating, that reflected so clearly the attributes of 'Abdu'l-Bahá's character; a sweetness of temper; a cheerfulness that no amount of sorrow could becloud; a quiet and unassuming disposition that served to enhance a thousand-fold the prestige of her exalted rank; a forgiving nature that instantly disarmed the most unyielding enemy – these rank among the outstanding attributes of a saintly life which history will acknowledge as having been endowed with a celestial potency that few of the heroes of the past possessed.

No wonder that in Tablets, which stand as eternal testimonies to the beauty of her character, Bahá'u'lláh and 'Abdu'l-Bahá have paid touching tributes to those things that testify to her exalted position among the members of their Family, that proclaim her as an example to their followers, and as an object worthy of the admiration of all mankind. (*Bahíyyih Khánum*, pp. 42–3)

He speaks of her as

Monument and grave of the Greatest Holy Leaf (Baker, 1933)

the 'well-beloved' sister of 'Abdu'l-Bahá, the 'Leaf that hath sprung' from the 'Pre-existent Root', the 'fragrance' of Bahá'u'lláh's 'shining robe', elevated by Him to a 'station such as none other woman hath surpassed', and comparable in rank to those immortal heroines such as Sarah, Ásíyih, the Virgin Mary, Fátimih and Táhirih, each of whom has outshone every member of her sex in previous Dispensations. (*God Passes By*, p. 347)

He adds that her 'services until the ripe old age of four-score-years-and-six, no less than her exalted parentage, entitle her to the distinction of ranking as the outstanding heroine of the

Bahíyyih <u>Kh</u>ánum, the Greatest Holy Leaf, daughter of Bahá'u'lláh (A portrait from life by Daisy Smythe, 1926)

Bahá'í Dispensation . . .' (ibid. p. 108)

Bahá'u'lláh Himself had honoured her, who was His favoured daughter, with a high tribute to her role and position in the Faith:

He is the Eternal! This is My testimony for her who hath heard My voice and drawn nigh unto Me. Verily, she is a leaf that hath sprung from this pre-existent Root. She hath revealed herself in My name and tasted of the sweet savours of My holy, My wondrous pleasure. At one time We gave her to drink from My honeyed Mouth, at another caused her to partake of My mighty, My luminous Kaw<u>th</u>ar. Upon her rest the glory of My name and the fragrance of My shining robe.

Let these exalted words be thy love-song on the tree of Bahá, O thou most holy and resplendent Leaf: 'God, besides Whom is none other God, the Lord of this world and the next!' Verily, We have elevated thee to the rank of one of the most distinguished among thy sex, and granted thee, in My court, a station such as none other woman hath surpassed. Thus have We preferred thee and raised thee above the rest, as a sign of grace from Him Who is the Lord of the throne on high and earth below. We have created thine eyes to behold the light of My countenance, thine ears to hearken unto the melody of My words, thy body to pay homage before My throne. Do thou render thanks unto God, thy Lord, the Lord of all the world.

How high is the testimony of the Sadratu'l-Muntahá for its leaf; how exalted the witness of the Tree of Life unto its fruit! Through My remembrance of her a fragrance laden with the perfume of musk hath been diffused; well is it with him that hath inhaled it and exclaimed: 'All praise be to Thee, O God, my Lord the most glorious!' How sweet thy presence before Me; how sweet to gaze upon thy face, to bestow upon thee My loving-kindness, to favour thee with My tender care, to make mention of thee in this, My Tablet – a Tablet which I have ordained as a token of My hidden and manifest grace unto thee. (*The Bahá'í World*, vol. v, p. 171)

'Abdu'l-Bahá, Whose constant friend and aid she was, had many times written to her in love and solace, in letters reflecting His knowledge of her rare endowments of heart and spirit.

Entrance to the Monument Gardens and Shrine of the Greatest Holy Leaf (Baker, c. 1935)

O my well-beloved, deeply spiritual sister! Day and night thou livest in my memory. Whenever I remember thee my heart swelleth with sadness and my regret groweth more intense. Grieve not, for I am thy true, thy unfailing comforter. Let neither despondency nor despair becloud the serenity of thy life or restrain thy freedom. These days shall pass away. We will, please God, in the Abhá Kingdom and beneath the sheltering shadow of the Blessed Beauty, forget all these our earthly cares and will find each one of these base calumnies amply compensated by His expressions of praise and favour. From the beginning of time sorrow and anxiety, regret and tribulation, have always been the lot of every loyal servant of God. Ponder this in thine heart and consider how very true it is. Wherefore, set thine heart on the tender mercies of the Ancient Beauty and be thou filled with abiding joy and intense gladness . . .

O thou my loving, my deeply spiritual sister! I trust that by the grace and loving-kindness of the one true God thou art, and wilt be, kept safe and secure beneath the sheltering shadow of the Blessed Beauty. Night and day thy countenance appeareth before mine eyes,

Shrine of Bahíyyih Khánum, the Greatest Holy Leaf (Baker, c. 1933)

and in my mind are engraved the traits of thy character . . .
(*Bahíyyih Khánum*, pp. 7, 9–10)

The Holy Mother: Munírih Khánum

On 30 April 1938, Munírih Khánum, the mother of 'Abdu'l-Bahá's children and His devoted wife for forty-eight years, passed away, she who, as a bright-faced and spirited girl, had come to marry the Master during His grim days of confinement in the prison city.

Shoghi Effendi cabled the news of her death to the Bahá'í world:

HOLY MOTHER MUNÍRIH KHÁNUM ASCENDED ABHÁ KINGDOM STOP WITH SORROWFUL HEARTS BAHÁ'ÍS WORLD OVER RECALL DIVERS PHASES HER RICH EVENTFUL LIFE MARKED BY UNIQUE SERVICES WHICH BY VIRTUE HER EXALTED POSITION SHE RENDERED DURING DARKEST DAYS 'ABDU'L-BAHÁ'S LIFE . . . (30 April 1938)

She, too, was interred in the gardens now lying below the arc, just west of the shrine of the Greatest Holy Leaf.

Tomb of Munírih Khánum, the wife of 'Abdu'l-Bahá

Development of the Monument Gardens

In 1939 Shoghi Effendi took the final steps which had long been in his mind to transfer the remains of the wife and son of Bahá'u'lláh to the base of the arc. He 'ordered in Italy twin marble monuments similar in style to the one he had erected' over the grave of the Greatest Holy Leaf. Then, in spite of obstacles raised by Covenant-breakers, he gained permission from the British authorities to exhume the two bodies for reinterment on Mount Carmel. Two days after that permission was given he went at daybreak to 'Akká cemetery and there, lovingly and with his own hands, removed the remains of Navváb to a new coffin, then proceeded to the Nabí Sálih cemetery to transfer Mihdí's dust to another new coffin, thereafter transporting both to the little house of the Minor Archives near the tomb of the Greatest Holy Leaf. Reporting this great step on 5 December 1939, he cabled: '. . . CHERISHED WISH GREATEST HOLY LEAF FULFILLED. SISTER BROTHER MOTHER WIFE 'ABDU'L-BAHÁ REUNITED ONE SPOT DESIGNED CONSTITUTE FOCAL CENTRE BAHÁ'Í ADMINISTRATIVE INSTITUTIONS AT FAITH'S WORLD CENTRE.' (*The Bahá'í World*, vol. viii, p 245)

Two vaults were cut from solid rock in the garden area and were carefully prepared for their precious occupants. Nineteen days later Shoghi Effendi placed the two coffins in the Shrine of the Báb, and the next day with the utmost reverence laid them in their spiritually fitting new homes. On 26 December he cabled: 'CHRISTMAS EVE BELOVED REMAINS PUREST BRANCH AND MASTER'S MOTHER LAID IN STATE BÁB'S HOLY TOMB. CHRISTMAS DAY ENTRUSTED CARMEL'S SACRED SOIL . . .' (ibid)[1]

Addressing the Bahá'ís throughout the West in one of his most significant statements on the future evolution of the World Centre, entitled *The Spiritual Potencies of that Consecrated Spot*, the Guardian wrote:

The Purest Branch, the martyred son, the companion, and amanuensis of Bahá'u'lláh, that pious and holy youth, who in the darkest days of Bahá'u'lláh's incarceration in the barracks of 'Akká entreated, on his death-bed, his Father to accept him as a ransom for those of His loved ones who yearned for, but were unable to attain, His presence, and the saintly mother of 'Abdu'l-Bahá, surnamed Navváb by Bahá'u'lláh, and the first recipient of the honoured and familiar title of 'the Most Exalted Leaf', separated in death above half-a-century, and forced to suffer the humiliation of an alien burial-ground, are

Twin tombs of Mírzá
Mihdí and his mother
Ásíyih Khánum, Navváb,
the wife of Bahá'u'lláh

now at long last reunited with the Greatest Holy Leaf with whom
they had so abundantly shared the tribulations of one of the most
distressing episodes of the Heroic Age of the Faith of Bahá'u'lláh.
(ibid. p. 247. The entire letter is reproduced on pp. 245–53.)

In 1944, further commenting upon the significance of this
action, he makes clear that

The conjunction of these three resting-places, under the shadow of
the Báb's own Tomb, embosomed in the heart of Carmel, facing the
snow-white city across the bay of 'Akká, the Qiblih of the Bahá'í
world, set in a garden of exquisite beauty, reinforces, if we would

correctly estimate its significance, the spiritual potencies of a spot, designated by Bahá'u'lláh Himself the seat of God's throne. It marks, too, a further milestone in the road leading eventually to the establishment of that permanent world Administrative Centre of the future Bahá'í Commonwealth, destined never to be separated from, and to function in the proximity of, the Spiritual Centre of that Faith, in a land already revered and held sacred alike by the adherents of three of the world's outstanding religious systems. (*God Passes By*, p. 348)

The Purest Branch: Mírzá Mihdí

The shrine of Mírzá Mihdí, the Purest Branch, stands beside that of his beloved mother Navváb, reflecting their closeness of spirit and also the love she bestowed through the years upon her younger son from his sickly childhood to his gentle and pious manhood. In the Tablets revealed by Bahá'u'lláh in the grievous hour of Mihdí's tragic passing He gives testimony to the youth's self-sacrifice and to his role in the establishment of the new Faith. These are quoted by Shoghi Effendi in the same significant letter:

'Upon thee, O Branch of God!' He solemnly and most touchingly . . . bestows upon him His benediction, 'be the remembrance of God and His praise, and the praise of all that dwell in the Realm of Immortality, and of all the denizens of the Kingdom of Names. Happy art thou in that thou hast been faithful to the Covenant of God and His Testament, until Thou didst sacrifice thyself before the face of thy Lord, the Almighty, the Unconstrained. Thou, in truth, hast been wronged, and to this testifieth the Beauty of Him, the Self-Subsisting. Thou didst, in the first days of thy life, bear that which hath caused all things to groan, and made every pillar to tremble. Happy is the one that remembereth thee, and draweth nigh, through thee, unto God, the Creator of the Morn'. . .

'Blessed art thou,' He, in another Tablet affirms, 'and blessed he that turneth unto thee, and visiteth thy grave, and draweth nigh, through thee, unto God, the Lord of all that was and shall be . . . I testify that thou didst return in meekness unto thine abode. Great is thy blessedness and the blessedness of them that hold fast unto the hem of thy outspread robe . . . When thou wast laid to rest in the earth, the earth itself trembled in its longing to meet thee. Thus hath it been decreed, and yet the people perceive not . . . Were We to recount the mysteries of thine ascension, they that are asleep would waken, and all beings would be set ablaze with the fire of the remembrance of My Name, the Mighty, the Loving.' (*The Bahá'í World*, vol. viii, pp. 249–51)

164

The Most Exalted Leaf: Ásíyih Khánum, Navváb

Among those who shared Bahá'u'lláh's exile was His wife, Ásíyih Khánum, the

saintly Navváb, entitled by Him the 'Most Exalted Leaf', who, during almost forty years, continued to evince a fortitude, a piety, a devotion and a nobility of soul which earned her from the pen of her Lord the posthumous and unrivalled tribute of having been made His 'perpetual consort in all the worlds of God'. (*God Passes By*, p. 108)

The station of Navváb is a high one, eliciting from both her supernal Husband and from her incomparable Son the most affecting tributes. The following are from the closing pages of the Guardian's letter:

Concerning the Most Exalted Leaf, the mother of 'Abdu'l-Bahá, Bahá'u'lláh has written: 'The first Spirit through which all spirits were revealed, and the first Light by which all lights shone forth, rest upon thee, O Most Exalted Leaf, thou who hast been mentioned in the Crimson Book! Thou art the one whom God created to arise and serve His own Self, and the Manifestation of His Cause, and the Day Spring of His Revelation, and the Dawning-Place of His signs, and the Source of His commandments: and Who so aided thee that thou didst turn with thy whole being unto Him, at a time when His servants and handmaidens had turned away from His Face . . . Happy art thou, O my handmaiden, and My Leaf, and the one mentioned in My Book, and inscribed by My Pen of Glory in My Scrolls and Tablets . . . Rejoice thou, at this moment, in the most exalted Station and the All-highest Paradise, and the Abhá Horizon, inasmuch as He Who is the Lord of Names hath remembered thee. We bear witness that thou didst attain unto all good, and that God hath so exalted thee, that all honour and glory circled around thee.'

'O Navváb!' He thus, in another Tablet, addresses her, 'O Leaf that hath sprung from My Tree, and been My companion! My glory be upon thee, and My loving-kindness, and My mercy that hath surpassed all beings. We announce unto thee that which will gladden thine eye, and assure thy soul, and rejoice thine heart. Verily, thy Lord is the Compassionate, the All-Bountiful. God hath been and will be pleased with thee, and hath singled thee out for His own Self, and chosen thee from among His handmaidens to serve Him, and hath made thee the companion of His Person in the day-time and in the night-season.'

'Hear thou Me once again,' He reassures her, 'God is well-pleased with thee, as a token of His grace and a sign of His mercy. He hath made thee to be His companion in every one of His worlds, and hath nourished thee with His meeting and presence, so long as His Name, and His Remembrance, and His Kingdom, and His Empire shall endure. Happy is the handmaid that hath mentioned thee, and sought thy good-pleasure, and humbled herself before thee, and held fast unto the cord of thy love. Woe betide him that denieth thy exalted station, and the things ordained for thee from God, the Lord of all names, and him that hath turned away from thee, and rejected thy station before God, the Lord of the mighty throne.'

'O faithful ones!' Bahá'u'lláh specifically enjoins, 'Should ye visit the resting-place of the Most Exalted Leaf, who hath ascended unto the Glorious Companion, stand ye and say: "Salutation and blessing and glory upon thee, O Holy Leaf that hath sprung from the Divine Lote-Tree! I bear witness that thou hast believed in God and in His signs, and answered His Call, and turned unto Him, and held fast unto His cord, and clung to the hem of His grace, and fled thy home in His path, and chosen to live as a stranger, out of love for His presence and in thy longing to serve Him. May God have mercy upon him that draweth nigh unto thee, and remembereth thee through the things which My Pen hath voiced in this, the most great station. We pray God that He may forgive us, and forgive them that have turned unto thee, and grant their desires, and bestow upon them, through His wondrous grace, whatever be their wish. He, verily, is the Bountiful, the Generous. Praise be to God, He Who is the Desire of all worlds, and the Beloved of all who recognize Him."'

And finally, 'Abdu'l-Bahá Himself in one of His remarkably significant Tablets, has borne witness not only to the exalted station of one whose 'seed shall inherit the Gentiles', whose Husband is the Lord of Hosts, but also to the sufferings endured by her who was His beloved mother. 'As to thy question concerning the 54th chapter of Isaiah,' He writes, 'This chapter refers to the Most Exalted Leaf, the mother of 'Abdu'l-Bahá. As a proof of this it is said: "For more are the children of the desolate, than the children of the married wife." Reflect upon this statement, and then upon the following: "And thy seed shall inherit the Gentiles, and make the desolate cities to be inhabited." And truly the humiliation and reproach which she suffered in the path of God is a fact which no one can refute. For the calamities and afflictions mentioned in the whole chapter are such afflictions which she suffered in the path of God, all of which she endured with patience and thanked God therefor and praised Him, because He had enabled her to endure afflictions for the sake of Bahá. During all this time, the men and women [Covenant-breakers] persecuted her in an incomparable manner, while she was patient, God-fearing, calm, humble and contented through the favour of her Lord and by the bounty of her Creator.' (*The Bahá'í World*, vol. viii, pp. 251–3)

The Monument Gardens at the foot of the arc: the tomb of the Greatest Holy Leaf is seen among the cypresses (right), the twin tombs of Mírzá Mihdí and Ásíyih Khánum, Navváb (left), and, partially concealed, the tomb of Munírih Khánum (centre).

With the establishment of the Monument Gardens the Guardian not only added a place of rare beauty but also created a spot which evokes poignant memories of those three exalted personages of the immediate family of the Manifestation who, in a major way, participated in the events of the critical years of the Heroic Age of the Faith when the Revelation of Bahá'u'lláh was born and later rooted in the Holy Land. Their combined years spanned the entire length of that age, and reached into the Formative Age in which we now live; it was the period which witnessed the completion of the Revelation, the ministry of its Exemplar, and the initiation by the Guardian of his global plans, plans which included gathering these blessed Tombs into a spot of ever-increasing potency.

The testimonies to them by Bahá'u'lláh, 'Abdu'l-Bahá and Shoghi Effendi will be the inspiration and guidance

For such as might undertake, in the days to come, the meritorious and highly enviable pilgrimage to these blessed shrines, as well as for the benefit of the less privileged who, aware of the greatness of their virtue and the pre-eminence of their lineage, desire to commune with their spirits, and to strive to acquire an added insight into the glory of their position, and to follow in their footsteps . . . (ibid. p. 249)

28　The International Bahá'í Archives

THE DEVELOPMENT of a Bahá'í archive for relics, precious manuscripts, and other priceless mementoes of the Faith began in 1929 with the completion of the last three rooms of the Shrine of the Báb, and by the end of the thirties included the small house at the east edge of the gardens near the Tomb of the Greatest Holy Leaf, respectively called the 'Major' and the 'Minor' Archives. In October 1952 the Guardian announced his decision to construct a second major edifice on Mount Carmel, the first to be placed on the great arc above the Monument Gardens. He commissioned its design and in October 1953 the approved design was shown to the Bahá'í world at the New Delhi Intercontinental Teaching Conference. The preliminary steps taken to begin construction are reflected in the Guardian's message of April 1954 to the Bahá'í world:

The design of the international Bahá'í Archives, the first stately Edifice destined to usher in the establishment of the World Administrative Centre of the Faith on Mt. Carmel – the Ark referred to by Bahá'u'lláh in the closing passages of His *Tablet of Carmel* – has been completed, and plans and drawings forwarded to Italy for the purpose of securing bids for its construction immediately after the conclusion of the necessary preliminary steps taken in the Holy Land for its forthcoming erection. (*Messages to the Bahá'í World*, p. 64)

Then the final obstacle in Haifa was overcome by the procurement of land essential to the project from an enemy of the Faith. Thus in November 1954 Shoghi Effendi joyfully announced that

The International Bahá'í Archives building as it neared completion. It lies at the western end of the arc on Mount Carmel. (1957)

The ownership of this plot will now enable us to locate the site, excavate the foundations, and erect the structure, of the International Bahá'í Archives . . . which will serve as the permanent and befitting repository for the priceless and numerous relics associated with the Twin Founders of the Faith, with the Perfect Exemplar of its teachings and with its heroes, saints and martyrs, and the building of which constitutes one of the foremost objectives of the Ten-Year Plan. (ibid. p. 74)

Construction was rapid and, despite many challenging details of artistry and technology, the Parthenon-like building was completed by Riḍván 1957, before the beloved Guardian passed to the Abhá Kingdom at the very time of purchasing furnishings for this his last creative endeavour. Thus it was left to Amatu'l-Bahá Rúḥíyyih Khánum[1] to follow out his instructions until the long room with its two balconies was filled with the items beyond value for which it had been created. Pilgrims now have the inestimable privilege of encountering, even for the brief moments allotted them in this beautiful museum of the Faith, physical objects which are tangible evidences of the great lives of its Founders, and also examples of Their Writings.

Shoghi Effendi himself described the precious contents of the International Archives of the Faith held in the Archives building:

These treasures include portraits of both the Báb and Bahá'u'lláh; personal relics such as the hair, the dust and garments of the Báb; the locks and blood of Bahá'u'lláh and such articles as His pen-case, His garments, His brocaded tájes (head-dresses), the ka<u>sh</u>kúl of His Sulaymáníyyih days, His watch and His Qur'án; manuscripts and Tablets of inestimable value, some of them illuminated, such as part of *The Hidden Words* written in Bahá'u'lláh's own hand, the *Persian Bayán*, in the handwriting of Siyyid Ḥusayn, the Báb's amanuensis, the original Tablets to the Letters of the Living penned by the Báb, and the manuscript of *Some Answered Questions*. This precious collection, moreover, includes objects and effects associated with 'Abdu'l-Bahá, the blood-stained garment of the Purest Branch, the ring of Quddús, the sword of Mullá Ḥusayn, the seals of the Vazír, the father of Bahá'u'lláh, the brooch presented by the Queen of Rumania to Martha Root, the originals of the Queen's letters to her and to others, and of her tributes to the Faith, as well as no less than twenty volumes of prayers and Tablets revealed by the Founders of the Faith, authenticated and transcribed by Bahá'í Assemblies throughout the Orient, and supplementing the vast collection of their published writings. (*God Passes By*, p. 347)

29 The Arc and the World Administrative Centre

AT THE CLOSE OF 1939 Shoghi Effendi, having realized his plan to develop the Monument Gardens, gave expression to his vision of what was to be created on Carmel's mountainside above those gardens.

. . . it must be clearly understood, nor can it be sufficiently emphasized, that the conjunction of the resting-place of the Greatest Holy Leaf with those of her brother and mother incalculably reinforces the spiritual potencies of that consecrated Spot which, under the wings of the Báb's overshadowing Sepulchre, and in the vicinity of the future Ma<u>sh</u>riqu'l-A<u>dh</u>kár, which will be reared on its flank, is destined to evolve into the focal centre of those world-shaking, world-embracing, world-directing administrative institutions, ordained by Bahá'u'lláh and anticipated by 'Abdu'l-Bahá . . . Then, and then only, will this momentous prophecy which illuminates the concluding passages of the *Tablet of Carmel* be fulfilled: 'Ere long will

God sail His Ark upon thee [Carmel], and will manifest the people of Bahá who have been mentioned in the Book of Names.'

To attempt to visualize, even in its barest outline, the glory that must envelop these institutions, to essay even a tentative and partial description of their character or the manner of their operation, or to trace however inadequately the course of events leading to their rise and eventual establishment is far beyond my own capacity and power. Suffice it to say that at this troubled stage in world history the association of these three incomparably precious souls who, next to the three Central Figures of our Faith, tower in rank above the vast multitude of the heroes, Letters, martyrs, Hands, teachers, and administrators of the Cause of Bahá'u'lláh, in such a potentially powerful spiritual and administrative Centre, is in itself an event which will release forces that are bound to hasten the emergence in a land which, geographically, spiritually, and administratively, constitutes the heart of the entire planet, of some of the brightest gems of that World Order now shaping in the womb of this travailing age. (*The Bahá'í World*, vol. viii, pp. 247–9)

Expatiating later upon the *Tablet of Carmel*, the Guardian clarified the significance of the 'Ark':

In this great Tablet [of Carmel] which unveils divine mysteries and heralds the establishment of two mighty, majestic and momentous undertakings – one of which is spiritual and the other administrative, both at the World Centre of the Faith – Bahá'u'lláh refers to an 'Ark', whose dwellers are the men of the Supreme House of Justice, which, in conformity with the exact provisions of the Will and Testament of the Centre of the Mighty Covenant is the body which should lay down laws not explicitly revealed in the Text. In this Dispensation, these laws are destined to flow from this holy mountain, even as in the Mosaic Dispensation the law of God was promulgated from Zion. The 'sailing of the Ark' of His laws is a reference to the establishment of the Universal House of Justice . . . (Translated from the Guardian's letter written in Persian to the Bahá'ís of the East – dated Naw-Rúz 111–1954)

In another message of this same year he elaborated the theme of the development and significance of the great complex of buildings soon to be erected on the mountain above the Monument Gardens:

These Edifices will, in the shape of a far-flung arc, and following a harmonizing style of architecture, surround the resting-places of the Greatest Holy Leaf, ranking as foremost among the members of her sex in the Bahá'í Dispensation, of her brother, offered up as a ransom by Bahá'u'lláh for the quickening of the world and its unification, and of their mother, proclaimed by Him to be His chosen 'consort in all the worlds of God'. The ultimate completion of this stupendous undertaking will mark the culmination of the development of a world-wide divinely-appointed Administrative Order whose beginnings may be traced as far back as the concluding years of the Heroic Age of the Faith.

This vast and irresistible process, unexampled in the spiritual history of mankind, and which will synchronize with two no less significant developments – the establishment of the Lesser Peace and the evolution of Bahá'í national and local institutions – the one outside and the other within the Bahá'í world – will attain its final consummation, in the Golden Age of the Faith, through the raising of the standard of the Most Great Peace, and the emergence, in the plenitude of its power and glory, of the focal Centre of the agencies constituting the World Order of Bahá'u'lláh. The final establishment of this seat of the future Bahá'í World Commonwealth will signalize at once the proclamation of the sovereignty of the Founder of our Faith and the advent of the Kingdom of the Father repeatedly lauded and promised by Jesus Christ. (*Messages to the Bahá'í World*, pp. 74–5)

Aerial photograph of the completed Seat of The Universal House of Justice (upper left at the apex of the arc), second of the buildings which together will comprise the administrative heart of the Bahá'í Faith. (1981)

The Seat of the Universal House of Justice

On 7 June 1972 the Universal House of Justice cabled to the Bahá'í world: '. . .ANNOUNCE ERE COMPLETION NINE YEAR PLAN DECISION INITIATE PROCEDURE SELECT ARCHITECT DESIGN BUILDING FOR SEAT UNIVERSAL HOUSE JUSTICE ENVISAGED BELOVED GUARDIAN ON FAR FLUNG ARC HEART MOUNT CARMEL . . .'

In September 1973 Ḥusayn Amánat of Írán was chosen as the architect for the Seat of The Universal House of Justice, a mighty edifice to be erected at the zenith of the arc. In February 1974 his design was accepted and with all speed the process of construction was set afoot, beginning with a massive excavation of the mountain face and proceeding rapidly, but with precision and attention to every detail, in order to erect a monumental building for the centuries. In its message of 5 June 1975 to the followers of Bahá'u'lláh throughout the world the Universal House of Justice emphasized the timeliness of the work:

The first of the majestic edifices constituting this mighty Centre, was the building for the International Archives of the Faith which was completed in the summer of 1957 as one of the last major achievements of Shoghi Effendi's Guardianship and which set the style for

the remaining structures which, as described by him, were to be raised in the course of time in the form of a far-flung arc on the slope of Mount Carmel. In the eighteen years since that achievement, the community of the Most Great Name has grown rapidly in size and influence; from twenty-six National Spiritual Assemblies to one hundred and nineteen, from some one thousand to seventeen thousand Local Spiritual Assemblies, and from four thousand five hundred localities to over seventy thousand, accompanied by a corresponding increase in the volume of the work carried on at the World Centre of the Faith and in the complexity of its institutions. It is now both necessary and possible to initiate construction of a building that will not only serve the practical needs of a steadily consolidating administrative centre but will, for centuries to come, stand as a visible expression of the majesty of the divinely ordained institutions of the Administrative Order of Bahá'u'lláh. (*The Bahá'í World*, vol. xvi, pp. 397–8)

Classical in its exterior and in harmony with the International Bahá'í Archives, the exterior of the building is graced by a colonnade of fifty-eight pillars; its marble skin is chosen to resist the weathering of a millennium; its interior is simple, open, and adaptable to the evolving functions of a long future in service to the Faith. Important for the pilgrim are the council chamber of the Universal House of Justice, the magnificent main hall and splendid library-banquet room, and also the building's commanding position high on Carmel's slope, yet still in the shadow of the jewel-like Shrine of the Báb.[1]

30 The Site of the Mashriqu'l-Adhkár in Haifa

IN THE CLOSING YEARS of His life Bahá'u'lláh repeatedly turned His gaze southward to the long mountain rearing above the then inconsequential town of Haifa, that mountain of the fugitive Prophet Elijah, the mountain called 'The Vineyard of God' by the Jews.

During the last of His three visits to Haifa, on a summer day in 1891 'when His tent was pitched in the vicinity of the Carmelite Monastery', 'Bahá'u'lláh summoned His amanuensis and then revealed, in a clear loud voice, the first portion of the *Tablet of Carmel*', 'remarkable for its allusions and prophecies'.[1] The 'forceful tone of His exalted language sounded all around, so that even the monks, within the walls of the monastery, heard every word uttered by Him. Such was the commotion created on that historical occasion, . . . the earth seemed to shake, while all those present were overpowered by His mighty and wondrous spirit.' (Giachery, *Shoghi Effendi*, p. 210, relating words of the Guardian)

In the course of that same day Bahá'u'lláh, 'Abdu'l-Bahá, local believers and Persian pilgrims visited the upper Cave of Elijah in the nearby Carmelite Monastery. It was a day of rare significance upon that mountain-top with its spectacular view in all directions: the Mediterranean to the west, Nazareth and

174

Mount Hermon to the east, the Ladder of Tyre[2] to the north and the Carmel and hills of Samaria southward. There where sea meets land and heaven the earth, there upon Elijah's mountain, the Prophet made cogent reference to the World Administrative Centre of the Faith so soon to come.

Mindful of the future need to have a great House of Worship befitting the Bahá'í World Centre, the Guardian sought the best site. The place he chose was not far from the western tip of the Carmel and the monastery. In April 1954 he announced:

The site for the first Mashriqu'l-Adhkár of the Holy Land has been selected . . . situated at the head of the Mountain of God, in close proximity to the Spot hallowed by the footsteps of Bahá'u'lláh, near the time-honoured Cave of Elijah, and associated with the revelation of the *Tablet of Carmel*, the Charter of the World Spiritual and Administrative Centres of the Faith on that mountain. (*Messages to the Bahá'í World*, p. 63)

In April 1955 he confirmed that

The international Bahá'í endowments on Mt. Carmel have been greatly enhanced by . . . the acquisition of an area of thirty-six thousand square metres, . . . to serve as the site for the first Mashriqu'l-Adhkár of the Holy Land, the entire sum having been donated by Amelia Collins, Hand of the Cause and outstanding benefactress of the Faith. (ibid. pp. 78–9)

Recognizing that construction of a Mashriqu'l-Adhkár would only occur long decades later, the Guardian commissioned in Italy the design and fashioning of an obelisk and had it shipped to the Holy Land. In August 1971 the obelisk was erected on the site by the Universal House of Justice as a symbol of the great Temple one day to rise there, and as a place of visitation for present-day pilgrims; a cablegram informed the believers:

JOYOUSLY ANNOUNCE FURTHER DEVELOPMENTS WORLD CENTRE. AFTER MANY YEARS DIFFICULT NEGOTIATIONS ERECTION OBELISK MARKING SITE FUTURE MASHRIQU'L-ADHKÁR MOUNT CARMEL COMPLETED THUS FULFILLING PROJECT INITIATED BELOVED GUARDIAN EARLY YEARS CRUSADE . . .

Mid-nineteenth century artist's view westward down the edge of the Carmel escarpment to the Stella Maris Monastery, from near the place where Bahá'u'lláh pitched His tent and revealed the *Tablet of Carmel*. (Oliphant, *Haifa*)

Aerial view of the obelisk on the site of the future Bahá'í Temple

Obelisk marking the site, near the western tip of Mount Carmel, of the future Mashriqu'l-Adhkár of the Bahá'í World Centre. The view is north-eastward, across the Bay of Haifa to the Galilee hills.

31 The Pilgrim House in Haifa

SOON AFTER the entombment of the remains of the Báb [in 1909], one of the believers from 'Ishqábád, Mírzá Ja'far Rahmání,[1] begged 'Abdu'l-Bahá to allow him to build a Pilgrim House in the precincts of the Shrine for the convenience of visiting pilgrims. The request was granted, and this believer personally supervised the construction work, and paid for all expenses.

Even before the Pilgrim House was completed, 'Abdu'l-Bahá gave a sumptuous banquet for the friends and pilgrims from East and West. When the construction was finished and the beloved Master entered the new building, Mírzá Ja'far Rahmání devotedly threw himself at His feet, drowned in tears of joy. 'Abdu'l-Bahá lovingly lifted him, and asked him to express any wish he had. Mírzá Ja'far did not reply, for his sole desire was to see his Master happy. However, one of the attendants of the Master, Hájí Mírzá Haydar-'Alí, surnamed 'Angel of Carmel' by the Master Himself, stepped forward and suggested that in acknowledgement of Mírzá Ja'far's services, the Master might permit an inscription to be incorporated in the building in his honour, and if He accepted the suggestion, would He write the words. The Master graciously agreed, and, with paper and pen hastily supplied, He wrote the words, in Persian, which now appear engraved on a stone above the entrance of the Pilgrim House. The translation is: 'This is a spiritual Hostel for Pilgrims, and its founder is Mírzá Ja'far Rahmání 1327 AH (1909 AD)' (*Bahá'í Holy Places*, pp. 85–6)

The Pilgrim House is a fine stone building which for decades was used to house the Eastern pilgrims, the side rooms serving as bedrooms for a number of these visitors, while the main hall, with its three graceful compartments and fine windows, was then a place for meeting.

During the ministry of 'Abdu'l-Bahá many meetings were held here in His Presence with the pilgrims and members of the local community. Later, when Shoghi Effendi became Guardian, he too met the assembled friends and talked to them in this Pilgrim House before leading them in prayer when visiting the Shrines of the Báb and of 'Abdu'l-Bahá. (ibid.)

In 1935, after demolition of the house of 'Azíz Sulaymán Dumit, a dwelling near the eastern edge of the Shrine property, a second stone building was erected near by as the Pilgrim House annex. In later years men pilgrims occupied one building, women the other.

In recent years many changes have been made to accommodate the increasing flow of pilgrims. Three families now live in the complex: the custodians of the Shrine occupy the smaller pilgrim building; the pilgrim hosts live in an adjacent apartment; the foreman of the gardens staff with his family occupies the lower level of the main building. At the time of the decision in 1969 to have pilgrims live in hotels, the main building was converted to a pilgrim centre, with library, tea-room, registration and projection-display rooms altered from what once

The dedicatory statement by 'Abdu'l-Bahá over the Pilgrim House doorway

were bedrooms. However, the central meeting-room with its three compartments continues unchanged, as a place for special celebrations and social gatherings, and which also functions as a focus of community life for World Centre staff, pilgrims and visitors.

The Pilgrim House in Haifa, built in 1909, now a centre of pilgrim activities, formerly the Eastern Pilgrim House

32 The Former Western Pilgrim House

FOLLOWING THE END of the First World War, the increasing number of Bahá'í pilgrims coming to the Holy Land created a need for more accommodation for pilgrims than that available at the time. The Pilgrim House for Eastern believers near the Shrine of the Báb was adequate, but that for Western pilgrims, a small stone dwelling across the lane (now Haparsim Street) from the Master's House, was unsatisfactory. One of the Persian friends offered 'Abdu'l-Bahá a piece of land located near by on the lane, a spot where once Bahá'u'lláh had pitched His tent. Then in November 1919 an American pilgrim, Mr William Harry Randall, asked if he might have the privilege of contributing a sum of money for the construction of a pilgrim house for the Western believers.

Both these offers were accepted and drawings were prepared under the Master's direction. Sketches for several possible designs were submitted, and one was chosen by Him as the most suited to the

No. 10 Haparsim Street, formerly the Western Pilgrim House, seat of The Universal House of Justice from 1963 to 1982 (Baker, 1926)

existing needs and climatic conditions. 'Abdu'l-Bahá Himself suggested certain changes in the arrangement of the proposed structure, and another sketch was prepared and presented to Him for further corrections and alterations. This process was continued until the final design was evolved and approved by the Master.

Subsequently construction of the building in accordance with this plan was begun, but the funds available proved insufficient and work on it was suspended until 1923, when the late Hand of the Cause Mrs. Amelia Collins came to the Holy Land as a pilgrim with her husband. The sight of the unfinished building led her to offer the funds necessary for its completion. This gift to the Faith was accepted by the beloved Guardian and the structure, when finished a few years later, became the Western Pilgrim House. (*Bahá'í Holy Places*, pp. 87–8)

The circular council chamber of the former seat of The Universal House of Justice at No. 10 Haparsim Street, to be occupied by the International Teaching Centre

The main hall, Western Pilgrim House, upon its completion (Baker, 1926)

In 1951 it became the seat of the International Bahá'í Council. And in 1963 the Universal House of Justice established its offices there.

During the period from 1963 to the time of completion and occupation of the Seat of The Universal House of Justice, the building has undergone remodelling in non-structural ways in order to adapt it for use as a facility for an expanding Secretariat. The handsome circular room at the northern end of the building has served as the council chamber of the House of Justice since 1963. The main hall has been used for meetings with pilgrims and for staff gatherings.

With the completion of the Seat of The Universal House of Justice it will become the office of the International Teaching Centre.

33 The Bahá'í Cemetery in Haifa

WHERE THE STEEP northern rock face of Mount Carmel plunges to the plain at the very tip of the promontory, and almost directly below the mouth of the lower Cave of Elijah, known as the School of the Prophets, lies the rectangular six-acre plot of the Bahá'í cemetery in Haifa. Allenby Road cuts along the base of the mountain at the southern edge, its construction and that of the apartment houses opposite the cemetery having shorn away cave tombs associated with the ancient village of Haifa.

Purchased at the behest of 'Abdu'l-Bahá, the cemetery's earliest recorded burial, in August 1911, was that of the first cousin of the Báb, Ḥájí Mírzá Muḥammad-Taqí Afnán, the Vakílu'd-Dawlih (Government Deputy). The early graves are clustered principally at the western edge of the enclosure; among their occupants are a number of distinguished believers mentioned in *Memorials of the Faithful*: Ḥájí Mírzá Muḥammad-Taqí Afnán, Ḥusayn Áqáy-i-Tabrízí, Ḥájí Muḥammad Khán and Muḥammad 'Alíy-i-Ardikání. Other devoted Bahá'ís buried here include Ḥájí Mírzá Ḥaydar-'Alí (d. 27 August 1920) and Ḥájí Mírzá Abu'l-Ḥasan Afnán and his wife, both of whom passed away in 1921.

The Bahá'í cemetery on Allenby Road, Haifa, as seen from Stella Maris Drive, with tombs of early believers (1), tombs of Hands of the Cause, members of the Universal House of Justice, and others (2), tombs of Bahá'ís interred in recent years (3), and the house of the caretaker (4).

In more recent decades the cemetery has been systematically beautified with hedges, palm-trees and floral plantings, even as further interments have occurred of loyal adherents dying in the Haifa–'Akká area. The tombs of the Hands of the Cause of God John E. Esslemont, Horace Holley, Amelia E. Collins,

Leroy C. Ioas, Ṭarázu'lláh Samandarí and Abu'l-Qásim Faizi, and also of Luṭfu'lláh Ḥakím and Amoz Gibson, members of the Universal House of Justice, are to be found here. Many zealous servants of the Faith are buried at the eastern edge of the cemetery; the contributions of some are summarized in the 'In Memoriam' sections of *The Bahá'í World* volumes.

With the development of Haifa's western approaches, two museums have been built on either side of the cemetery: to the west the Naval Museum combined with the Museum of Illegal Immigration and to the east the Maritime Museum. Within the cemetery's enclosure, walled on three sides, is a house for a caretaker family. The entry gate for pilgrims and visitors gives access from the eastern stairway.

34 The Caves of Elijah on Mount Carmel

The Upper Cave of Elijah and the Monastery of the Carmelite Fathers

FROM EARLY TIMES the high place of Mount Carmel's promontory had religious uses, doubtless for worship of a Baal Hadad of Carmel, according to the Roman historian Tacitus. By Roman times the worship of Zeus Carmelus Heliopolitanus apparently was conducted there. The upper cave is first mentioned by Byzantine writers in relation to a monastery with a quadrangular chapel built in the fifth or sixth century and destroyed by the Persians in AD 614; a sepulchral grotto was described as being carved out of the rock and, according to local legend, was called the Cave of Elijah,[1] which name may have been attached to it in Byzantine times when it was within the chapel. During the Arab period the chapel was given a mihrab, a prayer niche on the side facing Mecca, to convert it into either a maqám (shrine) or a small mosque. Visitors to the Holy Land during the Crusades described a Greek Abbey of St. Margaret (or St. Marina) of Mount Carmel on the terrace of the promontory, adjacent to the Templar fortress at its tip. The founding of the Carmelite monastic order occurred during the latter half of the Crusades, and since then the monks have been the builders and preservers of the churches and monasteries of the site.

As for the grotto itself, post-Crusader accounts tell of visitors entering the chamber from above to view Elijah's erstwhile stony bed. Seventeenth-century records of the quadrangular chapel which enclosed the grotto relate that first a window was cut into the chamber, then a doorway at its side, and finally the entire western rock face was removed, including the opening from above through which Elijah presumably descended to his hiding-place. A chapel was constructed by Giambattista in 1767–74, its high altar erected atop the grotto.

In 1799 a number of Napoleon's soldiers, wounded or sick with plague, were hospitalized in the monastery; about fifteen

Artist's view eastward to the Stella Maris Carmelite Monastery, in the latter part of the nineteenth century. Old Haifa is seen on the shore, 'Akká at the far horn of the bay. (Oliphant, *Haifa*)

184

of the plague victims were left behind upon his withdrawal, who, in panic at the coming of the Turkish soldiers, fled the hospital to die on the mountainside, and are now buried in front of the monastery. Destroyed by 'Abdu'lláh Páshá in 1821, both the church and monastery were rebuilt by Casini from 1827 to 1836; the present complex is called Stella Maris by common usage after the name earlier given to the nearby lighthouse. Interestingly, some Jewish and Muslim traditions associate the grotto with Elisha, disciple and successor of Elijah. Today, in addition to the occupation of the monastery by the Latin Carmelite Order, Greek Church members use the chapel for baptisms and worship, having customary rights dating back to Byzantine times but only recently renewed. The nearby building on the tip of the promontory is based upon a mansion constructed about 1823 by 'Abdu'lláh Páshá on the foundations of the Templar fort; in 1844 the Páshá sold the property to the monastery after his return from Egypt. In 1867 a lighthouse was built by a French company in association with the mansion; and for a long time the house also functioned as a hospice of the monastery until it was appropriated by the British and thereafter by the Israelis.

In Bahá'í historical associations the pitching of Bahá'u'lláh's

The cape of Mount Carmel. Note the Stella Maris Monastery and its pension atop the Carmel prior to the building of the lighthouse, and the buildings of the Lower Cave of Elijah (bottom right). (Carmel, Die Siedlungen, 1860s)

tent on Mount Carmel in the summer of 1891 brought Him to this spot of long and varied tradition. On this last visit to Haifa Bahá'u'lláh lived for about three months in the house of Elias Abyaḍ (now the Archbishop's Boarding School on Allenby Road). One day He went up the mountain to its promontory, and His tent was pitched a few hundred yards east of the Carmelite Monastery at a beautiful spot on what was then a bare and brushy mountain-top. On that day in 1891, Bahá'u'-lláh visited the monastery and doubtless the cave, thus hallowing the spot.

Impelled by the beauty and spiritual associations of the spot, as well as by His Prophet's vision of what was soon to come, at the tent site Bahá'u'lláh revealed the *Tablet of Carmel*. Befittingly, the House of Worship for the World Centre will be built just east of the tent site, at a spot now marked by an obelisk.

The Lower Cave of Elijah, called 'The School of the Prophets'

Shrouded in mystery is the ancient use of the cave near the base of the mountain at its western tip, a cave which had been carved from the chalky stratum at a chosen point. Elijah traditionally is said to have lived there. In Greek times it may have been a centre of worship of Adonis or of Tammúz (God of Green Things), and the cave was certainly used as the centre of a fertility cult as indicated by some 150 inscriptions, pagan graffiti in Greek scratched into the chalky walls, and dating probably to the second century BC in the Hellenic period. In Roman times Vespasian, then commanding general of the legions in the East during the war against the Jews, sacrificed here seeking auguries on his contemplated strike for imperial power; the signs were favourable here and elsewhere, and he became one of the soldier emperors. In Byzantine times, during the sixth century, the Greek Orthodox Monastery of Elijah was built at the site simultaneously with construction of the Abbey of St. Margaret on the cape above. A small church was built outside the lower cave during the Crusades. Christians have called it 'The School of the Prophets', a title acquired in some early century. During Arab times some new legends

Promontory of Mount Carmel from the north-west. At the top are seen the walls surrounding the Stella Maris Monastery and its pension; at the bottom the two buildings which flank the mouth of the lower Cave of Elijah. The building on the right was occupied by 'Abdu'l-Bahá in 1892, 1893 and later. (Getsinger, *c.* 1900)

The lower Cave of Elijah, known also as the 'School of the Prophets', a grotto carved from a chalky stratum at the foot of the cape of Mount Carmel. The grotto at the right is now occupied by orthodox Jews. (Bartlett, 1840)

were evolved concerning al-Khiḍr[2] (the Green or Immortal One), and both Druze and Arabs venerate the site.

Only in late centuries has there been any Jewish interest in the cave; however, there are neither Jewish inscriptions in and about the cave nor persistent ancient Jewish traditions applying to it, for Jewish attention has been concentrated upon the eastern face of Mount Carmel, at Mount Muḥraqá and the Spring of Elijah above the Kishon Valley where the great contest of Elijah with the priests of Baal almost certainly took place.

It is recorded by Mírzá Muḥammad-Javád-i-Qazvíní that Bahá'u'lláh visited the lower cave some time after His visit to the Carmelite monastery and cave, thereby also hallowing it for the generations to come.

Following Bahá'u'lláh's passing in May 1892, 'Abdu'l-Bahá came that summer to Haifa, living in the upper apartment of the western building near the cave mouth. There, in sorrow at the machinations of the Covenant-breakers and in relative isolation at this cool spot by the sea, the Master spent one month. Again in 1893 He sojourned at this same spot, as Bahá'í visitors signing the Carmelite Monastery registry recorded, and He stayed there in subsequent years.

Below left Entrance to the lower cave of Elijah, at the side of the eastern building

Below right The building w◄ of the lower cave of Elijah. 'Abdu'l-Bahá several times lived in the upper storey. The mouth of the cave is behind the building. (Getsinger, *c.* 1900)

35   The Society of the Temple

THE HOLY LAND has always been warmly held in the hearts of Christians of the western world, but their visions of that land have only rarely been as concretely realized as those of the action-motivated Protestant pietists of Württemberg in Germany of the mid-1800s.

One root of the pietist movement in Germany in the eighteenth century sprang from Revd J. A. Bengel, who predicted that the second coming of Christ would occur in 1837. However, this expectancy of the Return was not only fogged by disagreements on interpretation of the Scriptures, but ultimately was blunted by disappointment at the apparent failure of the prediction itself. Thus the founders of the Temple Society (Tempelgesellschaft), Christoph Hoffmann, Georg David Hardegg and Christoph Paulus, unhappy with the inadequacies of Christian society as they observed them, focused upon the concept of an ingathering of Christians in Jerusalem, where a dedicated community established by them would create 'a spiritual house' in the true spirit of Jesus Christ as called for by Paul in Ephesians,[1] and by Peter in his first Epistle.[2] In short, their dream was to establish a home of God, a Temple of God in the Holy City and widely throughout the Holy Land, although their former Adventist hopes were still alive within them. Dr Richard Hoffmann, the Head of the Temple Society,[3] has epitomized their goals in a contemporary statement:

The foundation members of the Temple Society were firmly convinced that the ills and the many crying needs of the time could be best overcome if the realization of the idea of God's kingdom on earth were to be attempted within the family and in simply organized, easily conducted communities. They hoped fervently that their formation of such communities, especially in the Holy Land, would stimulate Christianity at large to reconsider and adopt this early Christian principle of organization.

In 1858 Hoffmann, Hardegg and F. Bubeck came as scouts to survey the prospects for settlement in an inhospitable Turkish–Arab Muslim Palestine. After encountering grave difficulties they returned to Germany, but nevertheless in the early 1860s sent four young men as an advance group to prepare the way for the families then being recruited for the new adventure. Finally, Hoffmann and Hardegg themselves arrived in Haifa in October 1868, leading the wave of families which settled in several colonies during the period from 1868 to 1875, Hardegg remaining with the Haifa group, Hoffmann going to Jaffa. All firmly believed in the prophecies which foretold a glorious future for the Holy Land. Later settlements in the Galilee were at Bethlehem (Bet Lehem) near Tivon and at Waldheim, with a few families at Nazareth, Tiberias and, briefly, at Neuhardthof, north of Atlit. Near the early Jaffa–Walhalla colonies new settlements were established at Sarona and Wilhelma (now Bnei Atarot). The Jerusalem colony was established on the plain of Rephaim west of the city.

The first years were physically arduous ones, the settlers engaging in both farming and urban occupations, but they were also plagued by serious ideological conflicts and divisions within the communities. Nevertheless, through their worthy example and skilled services the Templers[4] were an important factor in the modern development of the Holy Land, so that they could look back upon many solid achievements when, in the late 1930s, the British Government resettled most of the families in Australia, some returning to Germany.

The German Templer colony, Haifa, looking down Carmel Avenue to the sea (Oliphant *Haifa*)

The Haifa colony, Society of the Temple, on the plain at the foot of Mount Carmel. The main street of the colony, then called Carmel Avenue, is seen as the axis of the settlement, running from the coast to the base of the mountain. (Carmel, *Die Siedlungen*)

The first and largest settlement was founded in Haifa under Hardegg's leadership in 1868–9, the immigrants constructing their village west of the old walled city on the fertile plain at the foot of Mount Carmel. The main street of the village extended from the base of the mountain to the beach of Haifa Bay, and was appropriately named Carmel Avenue; broad and tree-lined, the boulevard was worthy of the generous cut-stone homes of the Templers which faced upon it. About twenty-five of these homes reflected the religious dedication of their occupants through pious quotations carved into the stone lintels over their doorways. One house in particular, which fronts upon modern Hagefen Street, is adjacent to a spot where Bahá'u'lláh once pitched His tent, now a Bahá'í Holy Place. Over its erstwhile doorway, now a window, is the prescient inscription: 'Der Herr ist nahe 1871' (God is nigh 1871), inscribed by its builders, the family Pfander.[5]

It is known that Bahá'u'lláh spent some nights at what is now called Oliphant House (after Laurence Oliphant), one of

Hotel Carmel of the
Templer colony in Haifa at
the foot of Carmel Avenue,
in which the Master is
known to have stayed, and
probably Bahá'u'lláh also.
Note the Shrine of the Báb
on the mountainside.
(Carmel, *Die Siedlungen*,
1890)

the Templer buildings on Carmel Avenue, as well as in their inn near the sea. The Master had cordial relations with members of the colony, calling upon the skilled doctors of the group at times of sickness, and also upon certain Templers for assistance in business transactions involving acquisition of land on the mountain. The Templer Wilhelm Deiss not only planted the famous cypresses behind the Shrine of the Báb, but also sold his vineyard on the mountain to 'Abdu'l-Bahá, then became His gardener. The Guardian, as is recorded in *The Priceless Pearl*, appreciated his Templer neighbours for their solid virtues, myopic though they were with regard to the significance of the Faith and its fulfilment of Bengel's prediction.

The effective demise of the Templer settlements in the Holy Land occurred in 1948 with the coming of the State of Israel. However, the houses of these sturdy and devoted people are an abiding memento of their constructive presence for eighty years in a spot where their vision of a moral Christian community has been realized in a way which would astonish Christoph Hoffmann, were he alive in this hour.

The house of the Templer family Pfander (lower left), over whose doorway was inscribed the prophetic 'Der Herr ist nahe [God is nigh] 1871'. The circle of cypresses (lower right) marks the site of Bahá'u'lláh's tent which was pitched there in 1891. (*Insert*) The inscription over the original doorway, now a window facing on Hagefen Street.

193

Appendices

196

I Shaykh Maḥmúd 'Arrábí: Fanatic to Believer

THIS CHRONICLE is a combination of the stories from *The Chosen Highway, Bahá'u'lláh, The King of Glory*, and *'Abdu'l-Bahá*, and displays a sometimes arbitrary attempt to harmonize apparent inconsistencies of time and persons.

It was the time of Ramaḍán in the year 1850. The Shaykh and his family had fasted until sundown. Then they had their accustomed meal. When they had finished, my grandfather, then a little boy, cried out 'Look! Look! The sun is risen again, the sun has come back!'

The whole family stood looking at the western sky, where a brilliant gleam was shining. It seemed to them miraculous, after the darkness which was there when they sat down to break their fast.

My great-grandfather hurried to consult an old Shaykh who was a much-revered friend. In a state of great distress he related to his friend the episode of the seeming return of the sun, being full of anxiety lest he and his family should have broken the law which requires them to fast until the setting of the sun.

The aged Shaykh made answer:

'You have not broken the law, but a terrible crime has this day been committed in a far-off city of Persia; they have murdered the Mihdí, for whom we have been waiting, who has come to herald the coming of the "Great One" into this mortal world in fulfilment of the prophecies!

'Oh, the miserable blindness of man! How can such things be?'

On the next day the old Shaykh came to see my great-grandfather. He called the young son (my grandfather, Shaykh Maḥmúd) and said to him:

'Hearken unto me, my child:

'Unto this city of 'Akká will come one day the "Great One". He will abide in a high house with many, many steps. His sustenance will be provided by the Government [i.e., a prisoner]. Now thou wilt be here, in this city, when He cometh. I and thy father will have passed from this mortal world, but mark well what I now say unto thee:

A group of local friends and pilgrims gathered beneath the pines of Bahjí (1914)

197

'We charge thee to deliver the salutation of our hearts' devoted worship unto Him, mine and thy father's.'

My grandfather, Shaykh Maḥmúd, told us that, although still a child, his father and his friend, the old Shaykh, spoke often to him, charging him to keep this, their command, ever in his mind, and to obey 'when the time should have come'. . .

Time flowed on. The old Shaykh and my great-grandfather, Shaykh Qásim 'Arabí [sic], died, and my grandfather, Shaykh Maḥmúd, grew up into manhood, being always full of love and devotion to his religion, that of Islám. (Blomfield, *The Chosen Highway*, pp. 239–40)

In the year 1868 the news of the arrival of a party of dangerous heretics was noised about 'Akká; they were said to be enemies of Islám, and had been sentenced to exile and imprisonment in the unhappy city of 'Akká, led by the arch-heretic Himself, Who made preposterous claims for His position. Hearing the firman (decree) of Sultan 'Abdu'l-'Azíz read in the mosque, Shaykh Maḥmúd boiled with rage and was convinced that it was his duty to kill such an enemy of his beloved religion. Not being able to contain himself, he went to the gate of the citadel and demanded entry. As he was a prominent figure among the citizens of 'Akká, the guards did not refuse his demand and allowed him to enter, but told him that he would need permission to enter the presence of Bahá'u'lláh. Already armed with a weapon concealed beneath his 'abá (cloak), he requested permission to speak with the Prisoner. The reply came:

Interior stairs in the prison block which once gave access to the upper floor where Bahá'u'lláh was held now cut off below and blocked above by renovations. (*2 pictures*)

'Thou hast permission to approach when thou shalt have cast away thy weapon!'

Shaykh Maḥmúd was greatly astonished at the mention of the weapon, of which he had spoken to nobody.

My grandfather then said within himself, 'I am a strong man, I am able to kill this enemy by the strength of my hands, without the aid of a weapon.'

Again he sent his request to be received by the Prisoner. To which the reply came:

'When thou shalt have purified thy heart, then thou mayest come.'

Again my grandfather more greatly marvelled.

Then a dream came. The old Shaykh and his father appeared to Shaykh Maḥmúd and thus spoke to him:

'Go to the gathering-place of the friends of this Prisoner and say unto them:

'Alláh-u-Abhá.

'They will take no heed of thee at first, then say a second time:

'Alláh-u-Abhá.
'Still they will ignore thee.
'Then cry aloud for the third time:
'Alláh-u-Abhá.
'Now one will question thee: "What meanest thou by this word?"
Then shalt thou speak of our charge unto thee, years ago, to deliver
the salutations of our hearts' devoted worship.'

As he heard these words, the eyes of my grandfather, Shaykh
Maḥmúd, were opened, and he remembered all that the old Shaykh
and his own father, Shaykh Qásim 'Arabí, had said to him of the
'Great One' Who should come, even to 'Akká, and how He should
abide in a tall dwelling at the top of a long flight of steps.

My grandfather sought out the gathering-together place of the
friends of the Prisoner, the 'Most Great Prisoner'; he was allowed to
enter, and all things took place in accordance with the command
given in his dream.

The one Who said to him: 'What meanest thou by this word,
Alláh-u-Abhá?' was our beloved Master, 'Abdu'l-Bahá, through
Whom my grandfather, Shaykh Maḥmúd, was permitted to deliver
the salutation of their hearts' devoted worship, the old Shaykh's and
that of my great-grandfather, Shaykh Qásim 'Arabí, (ibid. pp. 240–
41)

Intense feelings and ingrained convictions die hard, and
Shaykh Maḥmúd had not yet come the full round of belief.
Thus, one day

he was present at a gathering where people were talking of 'Abdu'l-
Bahá as a good man, a remarkable man. The Shaykh could bear it no
longer and stormed out, saying that he would show up this 'Abbás
Effendi for what He was. In blazing anger he rushed to the mosque,
where he knew 'Abdu'l-Bahá could be found at that hour, and laid
violent hands upon Him. The Master looked at the Shaykh with that
serenity and dignity which only He could command, and reminded
him of what the Prophet Muḥammad had said: 'Be generous to the
guest, even should he be an infidel.' Shaykh Maḥmúd turned away.
His wrath had left him. So had his hate. All that he was conscious of
was a deep sense of shame and bitter compunction. He fled to his
house and barred the door. Some days later he went straight into the
presence of 'Abdu'l-Bahá, fell on his knees, and besought forgive-
ness: 'Which door but thine can I seek; whose bounty can I hope for
but thine?' (Balyuzi, 'Abdu'l-Bahá, pp. 33–4)

When Shaykh Maḥmúd had become both a friend and a
believer, although perhaps not declared as such, doubtless he
had frequent contact with the divine Prisoner until, on that dire
day of 23 June 1870 he was informed of the fall from the

barracks roof of Mírzá Mihdí, the Master's pious younger brother. Upon the youth's tragic death he requested of 'Abdu'l-Bahá

the honour of washing and shrouding the body of the Purest Branch, so that the guards should not lay their hands on that which was holy, and his offer was accepted; whereupon a tent was pitched in the yard, inside which the body of Mírzá Mihdí was laid, and with the aid of some of the companions . . ., who brought water and other accessories, Shaykh Maḥmúd washed and shrouded the body of the martyred son of Bahá'u'lláh for interment. (Balyuzi, *Bahá'u'lláh*, p. 313)

Thus prepared, the body went to its resting-place in the Nabí Ṣáliḥ cemetery.

Also, in those earliest days of difficult pilgrimage, when the great gates of 'Akká were closed at sundown,

Shaykh Maḥmúd used to go out into the countryside at night with a lantern and, whenever he encountered a Bahá'í come from afar and unable to gain entry into the city, he gave him the lantern to carry in front of him, as his servant; and thus he took the pilgrim into 'Akká, and into the citadel. And in the same way he would lead the pilgrim back to the safety of the countryside. (ibid. p. 338)

After the marriage of 'Abdu'l-Bahá to Munírih Khánum in 1872, Shaykh Maḥmúd attended to its recording in the Sharí'ah Court registry. Regrettably, during the brief fighting in 'Akká in 1948 the building containing the court records was burned, and this precious document was lost.

Another distinction came to the Shaykh during his long years of association with Bahá'u'lláh: in answer to a letter of request he received a Tablet which interpreted the Súrih of The Sun (xci, or No. xxiii in Rodwell's edition) revealed at Mecca as one of the first súrihs of the Qur'án. In this highly significant and unique work Bahá'u'lláh touches upon all fifteen verses of this brief súrih, framing His commentary with an opening sermon and a closing prayer. The commentary was printed in 1920 in Cairo in an early collection of His works.

When, in May 1892, there occurred the greatest sorrow, Bahá'u'lláh's ascension, it was again Shaykh Maḥmúd who requested the honour of washing the body of the Prophet. Together with the Master and the Bahá'í physician Khálid Jarráḥ, he paid his last homage to all that was mortal of 'The

Great One' Whom he had been destined to serve. Not content with the security of the burial room following the interment, and while the outer wall of the Shrine chamber was being reinforced and strengthened, Shaykh Maḥmúd kept watch in a tent set up next to the wall for the week required to complete the work of construction.

In the late 1890s Shaykh Maḥmúd 'Arrábí passed away, and he is buried in the Muslim cemetery of 'Akká, in his family area. No tombstone remains to mark the grave of this remarkable man, uniquely distinguished for his transition from learned Muslim fanatic to believer in Bahá'u'lláh.

II The Merchant 'Údí Khammár

AMONG THE POPULATION of 'Akká are Christians of Greek Orthodox, Maronite, Melchite and other denominations. Indeed in the nineteenth century as many as 5,000 Christians[1] were said to have inhabited the densely populated south-western quarter around the churches of St. George and St. Andrew. Two wealthy Christian merchants owned back-to-back houses at what is now called Genoa Square on the western edge of the middle city; one was 'Údí Khammár, the other Ilyás (Elias) 'Abbúd. Both were patrons of the Greek Orthodox Church of St. George.

'Údí Khammár (whose name means either 'the lute player and wine maker' or 'brewer of beer') was a successful merchant, first in grains and foodstuffs, later in wider business interests. Doubtless eager to escape the oppressive city, he purchased land north-east of 'Akká from Jirjis (Georges) and Iskandar (Alexander) Jamál. There he invested what must have been a great sum in restoring and enlarging the earlier building constructed by 'Abdu'lláh Páshá for his mother, producing a mansion of princely dimensions, the building surrounded by a small walled garden. Later a fringe of subsidiary houses was built by relatives to create a small colony; Naṣíf Ḥawwá' Khammár built the large apartment house north of the mansion. Over the doorway to the stairs leading to the upper and main floor 'Údí Khammár inscribed in Arabic the extra-

The Christian merchant 'Údí Khammár, whose two houses have achieved the greatest fame. Rebuilder of the Mansion of Bahjí, he was a patron of the Church of St. George and a relative of Ilyás 'Abbúd. This unsigned portrait was painted in Naples, 1876. (By permission of Faríd Khammár, 'Akko)

ordinary and prophetic verses about this house into which he had poured his fortune (see p. 107).

The restoration of this historic mansion corresponded with the period of Bahá'u'lláh's imprisonment in the barracks. In a Tablet to Mírzá Abu'l-Faḍl, Bahá'u'lláh referred to 'this lofty Mansion which had been built before the Manifestation and was raised when the Blessed Beauty entered the Most Great Prison'. After His ascension, Mírzá Áqá Ján wrote of Bahá'u'lláh's move to the Mansion at Bahjí 'which [was] transferred to Audeh ['Údí Khammár], the owner of the house in 'Akká, and he rebuilt the first floor, which was in ruins'.

By mid-1871 the family of 'Údí Khammár had moved to the Mansion of Bahjí just after the time when the mobilization of troops had required the emptying of the citadel to expand the barracks space. Thus, while Bahá'u'lláh and the Holy Family were being shunted through the three houses of Malik,[2] Khavvám, and Rábi'ih, the former city house of 'Údí Khammár became vacant and available for occupancy in September 1871.

At Bahjí 'Údí Khammár doubtless lived in the style of the educated and well-to-do Arab effendi, absorbing and reflecting much of the European culture which entered the city with merchants and travellers, and prospering with the commerce of what was still the best harbour town of the Palestinian coast.

In 1879 one of the recurrent violent epidemics struck 'Akká; very probably it was bubonic plague, a frequent visitor in this rat-infested port city, and the Khammár family fled from it, leaving Bahjí. Thus the noble mansion was empty to receive the Great Prisoner, then sojourning in the Mansion at Mazra'ih, and Khammár's son Andrávís[3] rented it to the Master. To it came Bahá'u'lláh for the last nearly thirteen years of His Mission. The Mansion was purchased by the Master some time before the Blessed Beauty's ascension.

During 1879 'Údí Khammár died and was buried in a room of the eastern housing complex, at the south-east corner of the mansion wall. In the later general demolition of the buildings which encrusted the splendid mansion, his tomb was preserved by the Guardian and the Hands of the Cause. One can enter the tomb room from the door in the southern wall, there to read the inscription in Arabic:

> Herein lies 'Údí Khammár who returned to his
> Lord and sought the abode of the righteous . . .

Ilyás (Elias) 'Abbúd,
Christian merchant of
'Akká, patron of the
Church of St. George,
friend of Bahá'u'lláh and
'Abdu'l-Bahá, d. 1878. This
unsigned portrait was
presumably painted in the
1870s. (By permission of
Faríd Khammár, 'Akko)

III   The Life of 'Abdu'lláh Páshá

AFTER THE DEATH of Aḥmad Páshá al-Jazzár in 1804, the Mameluke Sulaymán Páshá assumed power in 'Akká and further developed the city's trade and its physical resources. Among his other endeavours, Sulaymán completed a new aqueduct to replace al-Jazzár's aqueduct, damaged and ruptured during the siege of 1799 and whose stone had been robbed for new buildings.

In 1819 Sulaymán died and was buried in the courtyard of the al-Jazzár Mosque, to be succeeded as Páshá by nineteen-year-old 'Abdu'lláh, husband of his only daughter Fáṭimih and son of his former treasurer, the Mameluke 'Alí Páshá. 'Abdu'lláh soon put to death his able Jewish minister Haim Farhí, who had served both al-Jazzár and Sulaymán as their financial adviser, because he suspected a conspiracy with his Turkish overlords. 'Abdu'lláh's subsequent clash with the Sultan of Turkey was mediated by Muḥammad-'Alí, Viceroy of Egypt, so that he was both pardoned and confirmed in his post.

An ambitious and acquisitive young man, 'Abdu'lláh had inherited extensive lands along the course of the new aqueduct, at al-Bahja and Mazra'ih. He took over his wife's patrimony, Sulaymán's great estate and mansion outside 'Akká; this splendid house is known by the name of its last owners, the Baydúns, but is now an Israeli institution for the handicapped, the Atidot School. From his father he gained, near the hamlet of Mazra'ih, a fine summer house with enclosed garden, set in orchards, its terrace crossed by the channel of the aqueduct, its eastern windows looking outwards across the fertile valley to the hills with their highland Druze settlements. At the western tip of the Carmel he built a third mansion, whose structure forms a large part of the foundation of the present British–Israeli lighthouse. Early in his time of rule he occupied, as his Governorate, the buildings in the north-west corner of 'Akká which had been constructed *circa* 1810 by his father[1] on land obtained from Sulaymán. A mansion at the south-east corner of the walled enclosure of this 'Akká property was occupied by later governors. The Governorate itself was a two-storey broken square of buildings incorporating significant Crusader foundations in its northern segment.

'Abdu'lláh Páshá, throughout his stormy days as ruler of the area, had elevated ideas of his own merits, even going so far as to announce publicly, in the presence of the Muftí of Gaza, that he fulfilled in himself the conditions of the true Caliph. However, he was threatened by the power hunger of his dangerous neighbour to the south, Muḥammad-'Alí Páshá of Egypt. Some 10,000 Egyptians had fled the oppressive laws and military conscription of Egypt to settle upon the sparsely inhabited plain of southern Palestine, the Shefela, during the decades of Muḥammad-'Alí's rule. With this as a pretext, the Egyptian Páshá quarrelled with 'Abdu'lláh, and sent his son, Ibráhím, to invade Palestine in the autumn of 1831. The Egyptian army invested 'Akká for six months and took it in 1832 after a heavy bombardment which damaged or destroyed almost every building in the city. After the surrender 'Abdu'lláh was carried off to 'honorary' confinement in Egypt.

Eight years later the British[2] and Austrians, supporting the Turks in their reaction to Egypt's conquest, shelled the partially rebuilt city from the sea on 3 November 1840. A lucky hit found the ammunition magazine, killing many soldiers. Ibráhím Páshá, in Damascus when the fleet arrived off 'Akká, accepted the military defeat, retreated to Egypt, and the area reverted to direct Turkish rule. The city of 'Akká, seriously damaged by the two sieges, was indeed the sick and ugly plague spot which Bahá'u'lláh called 'the metropolis of the owl', and has never fully recovered from the two nineteenth-century attacks upon it.

When freed by Egypt, 'Abdu'lláh Páshá returned to the Haifa–'Akká area, sold the Stella Maris monastery back to its monks and sought to recoup his other properties. He then went to Constantinople, and finally to the Ḥijáz, where he died.

IV   Bahá'í Properties in the Galilee and Jordan Valley

WHEN BAHÁ'U'LLÁH and the Master set afoot the movement of the exiles from the immediate environs of 'Akká, land was purchased in the Jordan Valley near the Sea of Galilee (Lake Kinneret). At four sites Bahá'ís settled, making their homes.[1]

South of the hamlet called Nuqayb, on the eastern shore of the lake below the Golan heights, Mírzá Muḥammad-Qulí and his family occupied rich farmlands. The original large tract of land was purchased for an endowment of the Faith and registered in the name of Mírzá Ḥusayn-'Alí (Bahá'u'lláh). Later,

The loyal half-brother of Bahá'u'lláh, Mírzá Muḥammad-Qulí, as a young man holding one of his children (1868), and as an old man (c. 1900)

portions were disposed of by the Master. Finally, with the formation of the Israeli Kibbutz Ein Gev close by, and in 1948 with the fixing of the dangerous Syrian border overhead near the edge of the Golan escarpment, the several Bahá'í families left the area. On 12 November 1952 the land still held by the family of Mírzá Muḥammad-Qulí was exchanged with the Israel Government for an acreage at Bahjí, thus accounting for a large proportion of the present area at that Holiest Site.

When Mírzá Muḥammad-Qulí passed away in 1910 in Samras, his body was transported to the lakeside at Nuqayb for interment. 'Abdu'l-Bahá, in an obituary prayer, mourned for 'my old companion and affectionate comforter, my illustrious uncle' who, repairing to 'God's sublime kingdom', had entered 'the midmost heart of the exalted Paradise . . .' In a later Tablet the Master was consoled that 'his resting-place stands . . . in a beautiful garden among meadows [at] the seaside, the pleasant garden and the place . . . surrounded by trees and flowers. Its charm and beauty are indescribable.' The tiny cemetery at the lake holds not only the remains of Mírzá Muḥammad-Qulí, but also those of his son Dhikru'lláh and eleven relatives. The cemetery has been moved to a site near by at the foot of Tell Susita (Hippos).

Several of the families related to Mírzá Muḥammad-Qulí farmed land south of their childhood home, in a small settlement called Samras, or Samrih. With the onset of war in 1948 they left the area, and the hamlet has now disappeared into the banana and date-palm groves of the kibbutzim.

'Samakh, now called Zemah, was a station on the Haifa–Damascus railroad, and was situated at the south-east curve of the lake. Here for eight years lived the Bahá'ís, Ṣaláḥ al-Dín Jarráḥ and his mother, during which time Mr Jarráḥ served as postmaster for an extensive area including the strong kibbutzim Degania A and B, and Afikim.

At the southern base of the Golan and through the gorge which separates it from the mountains of Gil'ad (Gilead) flows the Yarmuk River. Where it leaves the hills, diagonally crossing the plain to join the Jordan River, stands the village of 'Adasíyyih, its fields stretching westward into the fertile alluvium of the valley, its grazing lands extending eastward up the hill-slopes. Here settled nearly thirty Bahá'í families, originally on land owned by 'Abdu'l-Bahá. At one time the community of Bahá'ís comprised much of the village population; they were

Das Deutsche (Grossmann) Hotel of the Templers in Tiberias, now a youth hostel. 'Abdu'l-Bahá stayed in the upper room with balcony, below the hotel sign. (Carmel, *Die Siedlungen*, c. 1925)

208

served by a fine local Ḥaẓíratu'l-Quds and were visited by the Master on a number of occasions. After 1948, when the border of the Kingdom of Jordan was established on the Yarmuk River, continuing local hostilities until the late 1960s finally induced the Bahá'ís to take refuge elsewhere in Jordan and Lebanon, and the Ḥaẓíratu'l-Quds is said to have been destroyed about 1970 by shellfire during what in Israel is called the War of Attrition.

'Abdu'l-Bahá had given the Bahá'í farmers specific guidance in their agricultural development, and His instructions on the storage of grains allowed the accumulations which permitted Him to feed the population of 'Akká during the deprivation of World War I and even to aid the British army in meeting its needs in 1918.

The family of Mírzá Muḥammad-Qulí, the most distinguished among the Galilee Bahá'í settlers, was given a further distinction among the believers for, when surnames were required of all families by the Turkish government, some of his descendants petitioned the Master to be allowed to take the family name of 'Bahá'í'. This they were permitted to do, and the family is now marked among the faithful by this tribute to their lineage, their unswerving loyalty and many services.[2]

The Master came to Tiberias on a number of occasions, often staying at the old Grossmann Hotel (Das Deutsche Hotel) next

to the Scottish Presbyterian Mission Hospital (the former now become a youth hostel, the latter a tourist pension), and once visiting the Muftí of Tiberias in his lakeshore home. He often visited the historic hot springs south of the city where once was the Biblical town of Hammath, or Rakkath. He is known to have gone, also, to the Hammat Gader, the hot springs up the Yarmuk River east of 'Adasíyyih, a spot frequented by the ailing for many centuries; the ruins of the Roman bath have recently been excavated and the entire area is being developed as a park and spa.

V The Druze of Israel

WHO WERE the friendly Druze of the western Galilee and Mount Carmel who were visited by Bahá'u'lláh and by 'Abdu'l-Bahá, and who sheltered the Bahá'í community during the early months of World War I? What are their beliefs and what is known about them?

The Druze emerge into history in the time of the sixth Fáṭimid Caliph of Egypt, al-Ḥákim (AD 985–1021, AH 375– 411), who ruled Egypt when the Ismá'ílí Shí'ih doctrines of Islám were the official belief of that land. Al-Ḥákim's reign was troubled, particularly since he put forth ideas differing strongly from prevailing Ismá'ílí theology, he himself claiming to be the incarnation and manifestation of God, the One. Ḥamzih, his principal disciple, and al-Darazi (al-Daraz'iyyih 'the tailor', from whom the name of the movement derives) were active teachers of the new doctrines during al-Ḥákim's lifetime. The Caliph, however, disappeared in AD 1021 (AH 411),[1] without having used the power of the caliphate either to establish his faith or to suppress opposition to it, and in Egypt the effect of al-Ḥákim's heterodoxy was short-lived. In Syria, however, to which some of his followers fled, a number of peasants in the mountains were converted and these communities have, over

210

stormy centuries of conflict, during which time they became famed as warriors, retained their communal integrity and beliefs, and have grown until they now number perhaps 300,000 members in Syria, the Lebanon, and Israel.

Their religious tenets have been held as secrets, and even within Druze communities only the sages know the teachings in their details of theology, cosmology and eschatology, while the people know only the common principles: to believe in one God and in al-Ḥákim as the Lord, to obey his precepts, to speak truth among the faithful, to defend and aid one another, and to dissociate oneself from unbelievers. There is a belief in the coming again of al-Ḥákim in a thousand years. And, among others revered for their historical roles, the father-in-law of Moses, Jethro (Nabí Shuʿayb), is given a high place in doctrinal history; his traditional tomb near Tiberias at the foot of the Horns of Hittin is a place of pilgrimage and of spiritual retreat. Some Muslim scholars consider the Druze as the most extreme of the Ismáʿílí sects, while the Druze consider themselves an independent religion.[2]

In Israel there are perhaps 50,000 Druze, whose settlements are found on the Carmel and in the Galilee hills, often in high and defensible sites, settlements whose population frequently is of mixed Christian, Muslim and Druze families. With the Six Day War and Israel's conquest of the Golan, a number of Hauran Druze who have lived for many generations at the foot of Mount Hermon also have come under the Israeli Government.

A Brief Chronology of Key Bahá'í Events in the Holy Land

Ministry of Bahá'u'lláh

31 August 1868	Arrival of Bahá'u'lláh with the company of exiles
23 June 1870	Martyrdom of Mírzá Mihdí in the prison
4 November 1870	Bahá'u'lláh's removal from the prison to three successive houses within 'Akká
September 1871	Bahá'u'lláh's confinement in the House of 'Údí Khammár
August–September 1872	Marriage of 'Abdu'l-Bahá and Munírih Khánum
1873 et seq.	Bahá'u'lláh's revelation of the Kitáb-i-Aqdas, the Book of Laws, and thereafter the revelation of His Tablets related to the Aqdas
Late 1873	Bahá'u'lláh's occupation of the House of 'Abbúd
Early June 1877	Bahá'u'lláh's departure from the prison city for the Mansion of Mazra'ih and His first visits to the Riḍván Garden
September 1879	Bahá'u'lláh's occupation of the Mansion of Bahjí
1883	Bahá'u'lláh visits Haifa
1886	Passing of Ásíyih Khánum, entitled Navváb, in 'Akká
1887	Passing of Mírzá Músá, entitled Áqáy-i-Kalím, in 'Akká
Spring 1890 and Summer 1891	Bahá'u'lláh visits Haifa twice, pitches tent on Mount Carmel, reveals Tablet of Carmel and points to site of the future Shrine of the Báb
1891	Bahá'u'lláh reveals the Epistle to the Son of the Wolf
29 May 1892	Passing of Bahá'u'lláh and His burial at Bahjí. Nine days later His Will and Testament appointing 'Abdu'l-Bahá as Successor was unsealed and read at Bahjí

Ministry of 'Abdu'l-Bahá

circa October 1896	Occupation of the House of 'Abdu'lláh Páshá by 'Abdu'l-Bahá and family
1 March 1897	Birth of Shoghi Effendi, first-born of Díyá'íyyih Khánum and Mírzá Hádí Shírází Afnán, at the House of 'Abdu'lláh Páshá
10 December 1898	First western pilgrims arrive at the House of 'Abdu'lláh Páshá
31 January 1899	Holy Remains of the Blessed Báb secretly arrive in 'Akká and are concealed in the House of 'Abdu'lláh Páshá
20 August 1901	Confinement reimposed upon 'Abdu'l-Bahá by the Turkish Government
July–August 1908	'Abdu'l-Bahá freed as a result of the Revolution of the Young Turks
21 March 1909	Holy Remains of the Blessed Báb interred in the Shrine on Mount Carmel
1909–10	'Abdu'l-Bahá moves from 'Akká to Haifa
August 1910	'Abdu'l-Bahá leaves the Holy Land for Egypt, Europe and North America
5 December 1913	'Abdu'l-Bahá returns to the Holy Land
1914–15	Bahá'í community moves to shelter in the Druze village of Abú-Sinán at the beginning of World War I
March–April 1916 and February–March 1917	Tablets of the Divine Plan revealed by 'Abdu'l-Bahá
1918	Graduation of Shoghi Effendi from the Syrian Protestant College (American University of Beirut); becomes secretary of 'Abdu'l-Bahá
27 April 1920	Knighthood conferred on 'Abdu'l-Bahá by British authorities
October 1920–January 1921	Entrance of Shoghi Effendi to Balliol College, Oxford University, England
28 November 1921	Passing of the Master in Haifa

Ministry of Shoghi Effendi

3 and 7 January 1922	Will and Testament of 'Abdu'l-Bahá read in Haifa, the second time in the Master's House, designating Shoghi Effendi as the Centre of the Cause, and his

	assumption thereafter of the duties of the Guardianship
27 November 1929	Return of Bahjí to Shoghi Effendi from the hands of the Covenant-Breakers
July 1932	Passing of the Greatest Holy Leaf; her burial in the Monument Gardens, Haifa
25 March 1937	Marriage of Shoghi Effendi to Miss Mary Maxwell, Rúḥíyyih Khánum, later entitled Amatu'l-Bahá
30 April 1938	Passing of Munírih Khánum, the wife of 'Abdu'l-Bahá
Christmas period 1939	Reinterment of remains of Navváb and Mírzá Mihdí, mother and brother of 'Abdu'l-Bahá, in the Monument Gardens, Haifa
1944–9	Initial plans for the superstructure of the Shrine of the Báb to the beginning of construction
9 January 1951	Appointment of the International Bahá'í Council
24 December 1951	Naming of first contingent of twelve Hands of the Cause of God
29 February 1952	Naming of second contingent of seven Hands of the Cause of God
12 November 1952	Great expansion of the property holdings surrounding the Shrine of Bahá'u'lláh and the Mansion at Bahjí
Riḍván 1953	Inauguration of the world-wide Ten Year Crusade
October 1953	Completion of the superstructure of the Shrine of the Báb
1954–7	Construction of the International Bahá'í Archives
June 1957	Full retrieval of Bahjí from the Covenant-breakers
October 1957	Naming of the third contingent of eight Hands of the Cause of God
4 November 1957	Passing of Shoghi Effendi in London; interment in the New Southgate Cemetery, London
	(See Rabbani, *The Priceless Pearl*, pp. 455–62, for a detailed chronology.)

Custodianship of the Hands of the Cause of God

November 1957	First Conclave of the Hands of the Cause at Bahjí; nine Hands of the Cause chosen to serve as Custodians of the Bahá'í World Faith residing in the Holy Land

Riḍván 1961	Election of the International Bahá'í Council
Riḍván 1963	First International Bahá'í Convention in Haifa for election of The Universal House of Justice
	Conclusion of the Ten Year Crusade
	Bahá'í World Congress in London

The Universal House of Justice

Riḍván 1964	Launching of the Nine Year Plan
Riḍván 1968	Second election of The Universal House of Justice
21 June 1968	Establishment of the Continental Boards of Counsellors
7 June 1972	Decision to build the Seat of The Universal House of Justice
Naw-Rúz 1973	Acquisition by purchase of the Mansion of Bahá'u'lláh at Mazra'ih
Riḍván 1973	Third election of The Universal House of Justice
	Conclusion of the Nine Year Plan
	Publication of the *Synopsis and Codification of the Laws and Ordinances of the Kitáb-i-Aqdas*
	Publication of the Constitution of The Universal House of Justice
5 June 1973	Establishment of the International Teaching Centre
Riḍván 1974	Launching of the Five Year Plan
14 January 1975	Acquisition by purchase of the House of 'Abdu'lláh Páshá in 'Akká
Riḍván 1978	Fourth election of The Universal House of Justice
Riḍván 1979	Conclusion of the Five Year Plan
	Launching of the Seven Year Plan
End of 1982	Completion of the Seat of The Universal House of Justice

Bibliography

'ABDU'L-BAHÁ. *Memorials of the Faithful.* Translated and annotated by Marzieh Gail. Wilmette, Illinois: Bahá'í Publishing Trust, 1971.

—— *Selections from the Writings of 'Abdu'l-Bahá.* Compiled by the Research Department of the Universal House of Justice. Translated by a Committee at the Bahá'í World Centre and by Marzieh Gail. Haifa: Bahá'í World Centre, 1978.

—— *The Secret of Divine Civilization.* Translated by Marzieh Gail in consultation with Ali-Kuli Khan. Wilmette, Illinois: Bahá'í Publishing Trust, 1970.

AURA, IBRAHIM. *The History of the Governorship of Sulayman Pasha, the Man of Justice.* With accompanying documents. Press of the Convent of Mukhales, 1936.

Bahá'í Holy Places. Haifa: Bahá'í World Centre, 1968.

Bahá'í World, The. An International Record.

Vol. V. 1932–34. New York: Bahá'í Publishing Committee, 1936.

Vol. VIII. 1938–40. Wilmette, Illinois: Bahá'í Publishing Committee, 1942. © 1942 National Spiritual Assembly of the Bahá'ís of the United States and Canada.

Vol. XII. 1950–54. Wilmette, Illinois: Bahá'í Publishing Trust, 1956.

Vol. XIII. 1954–63. Haifa: Bahá'í World Centre, 1970.

Vol. XV. 1968–73. Haifa: Bahá'í World Centre, 1976.

Vol. XVI. 1973–76. Haifa: Bahá'í World Centre, 1978.

BAHÁ'U'LLÁH. *Epistle to the Son of the Wolf.* Translated by Shoghi Effendi. Wilmette, Illinois: Bahá'í Publishing Trust, rev. edn 1976.

—— *Tablets of Bahá'u'lláh Revealed after the Kitáb-i-Aqdas.* Translated by Habib Taherzadeh with assistance of a Committee at the Bahá'í World Centre. Haifa: Bahá'í World Centre, 1978.

BAHÍYYIH KHÁNUM. The Greatest Holy Leaf. A compilation from Bahá'í sacred texts and writings of the Guardian of the Faith and Bahíyyih Khánum's own letters. Haifa: Bahá'í World Centre, 1982.

BALYUZI, H. M. *'Abdu'l-Bahá. The Centre of the Covenant of Bahá'u'lláh.* Oxford: George Ronald, 1973.

—— *Bahá'u'lláh, The King of Glory.* Oxford: George Ronald, 1980.

—— *Khadíjih Bagum, The Wife of the Báb.* Oxford: George Ronald, 1981.

BLOMFIELD, LADY. *The Chosen Highway.* Wilmette, Illinois: Bahá'í Publishing Trust, 1967. All rights reserved.

BROWNE, E. G. *Materials for the Study of the Bábí Religion.* Cambridge University Press, 1961. (For 'An Epitome of Bábí and Bahá'í History to AD 1898', translated from the Arabic of Mírzá Muḥammad Jawád of Qazwín, pp. 1–112.)

—— (ed.). *A Traveller's Narrative written to illustrate the Episode of the Báb.* Vol. II. Cambridge University Press, 1891.

CARMEL, ALEX. *Die Siedlungen der Württembergischen Templer in Palästina 1868–1918.* Stuttgart: W. Kohlhammer Verlag, 1973.

CHASE, THORNTON. *In Galilee.* Chicago: Bahá'í Publishing Society, 1921.

CHEYNE, T. K. *The Reconciliation of Races and Religions.* London: Adam & Charles Black, 1914.

DICHTER, B. *The Maps of Acre: An Historical Cartography.* Acre: Municipality of Acre, 1973.

ESSLEMONT, J. E. *Bahá'u'lláh and the New Era.* Wilmette, Illinois: Bahá'í Publishing Trust, 4th rev. edn (paper), 1976. © 1970, 1975 National Spiritual Assembly of the Bahá'ís of the United States.

FORD, MARY HANFORD. 'An Interview with 'Abdu'l-Bahá.' *Star of the West.* Vol. XXIV, No. 4, pp. 103–7, 1933.

FRIEDMAN, ELIAS. *The Latin Hermits of Mount Carmel: A Study in Carmelite Origins.* Rome: Institutum Historicum Teresianum, 1979.

—— *The Medieval Abbey of St. Margaret of Mount Carmel.* Rome: Ephemerides Carmeliticae XII, Teresianum, 1971.

GIACHERY, UGO. *Shoghi Effendi – Recollections.* Oxford: George Ronald, 1973.

GOLDMANN, ZE'EV. 'An 11th Century Arab Doorway in Old Akko.' *Teva va-Aretz* (Israel – Land and Nature). Vol. 2, No. 3, April 1977.

GOODALL, HELEN S. and ELLA GOODALL COOPER. *Daily Lessons Received at Acca, January, 1908.* Chicago: Bahá'í Publishing Society, 1908.

MCNEILL, LILIAN. 'Treasured Memories.' *World Order.* Vol. IV, No. 10, pp. 383–5, January 1939.

MAKHOUL, NAJI HABIB. *'Akka and Its Villages.* 'Akka: Office of Al Aswar, 1979.

MAKHOULY, N. and C. N. JOHNS. *Guide to Acre.* Jerusalem: Government of Palestine, 2nd edn, 1946.

MOMEN, MOOJAN. *The Bábí and Bahá'í Religions, 1844–1944.* Oxford: George Ronald, 1981.

MUNÍRIH KHÁNUM. *Episodes in the Life of Moneereh Khanum.* Translated by Ahmad Sohrab. Los Angeles: Persian–American Publishing Co., 1924.

OLIPHANT, LAURENCE. *Haifa, or Life in the Holy Land, 1882–1885.* New edn and introduction by Rechavam Zeevy. Jerusalem: Canaan Publishing House, 1976.

RABBANI, RÚHÍYYIH. *The Priceless Pearl.* London: Bahá'í Publishing Trust, 1969.

RODWELL, REVD J. M. *The Koran.* Everyman's Library. London: J. M. Dent & Sons, 1909.

RUSTAM, ASAD J. *Notes on 'Akka and Its Defences under Ibrahim Pasha.* (Probably Beirut: American Press), 1936.

—— *The Royal Archives of Egypt and the Origins of the Egyptian Expedition to Syria 1831–1841.* Beirut: American Press, 1936.

SHOGHI EFFENDI. *The Advent of Divine Justice.* New York: Bahá'í Publishing Committee, 1939.

—— *God Passes By.* Wilmette, Illinois: Bahá'í Publishing Trust, 1965.

—— *Guidance for Today and Tomorrow.* A Selection from the Writings of Shoghi Effendi. London: Bahá'í Publishing Trust, 1953.

—— *Messages to the Bahá'í World, 1950–1957.* Wilmette, Illinois: Bahá'í Publishing Trust, 1958.

—— and SITÁRIH KHÁNUM (Lady Blomfield). *The Passing of 'Abdu'l-Bahá.* Stuttgart: 1922.

—— *The Spiritual Potencies of That Consecrated Spot.* New York: Bahá'í Publishing Committee, 1940. (Reprinted in *The Bahá'í World*, Vol. VIII, and in White, *A Compendium of Volumes of The Bahá'í World*, I–XII.)

—— *The World Order of Bahá'u'lláh.* Wilmette, Illinois: Bahá'í Publishing Trust, 1980.

Star of the West. The Bahá'í Magazine.

—— Vol. XII (1921–2). Chicago: Bahá'í News Service. Reprinted in *Star of the West.* Vol. 7. Oxford: George Ronald, 1978.

—— Vol. XXIV (1933–4). Washington, D.C.: National Spiritual Assembly of the Bahá'ís of the United States and Canada.

Synopsis and Codification of the Laws and Ordinances of the Kitáb-i-Aqdas. Haifa: Bahá'í World Centre, 1973.

TAHERZADEH, ADIB. *The Revelation of Bahá'u'lláh.*

—— Vol. 1. Oxford: George Ronald, 1974.

—— Vol. 2. Oxford: George Ronald, 1977.

WHITE, ROGER (ed.). *A Compendium of Volumes of The Bahá'í World.* An International Record. Vols. I–XII. Oxford: George Ronald, 1981.

World Order. Vol. IV (1938–9). New York: World Order.

Notes

Details of titles mentioned in these Notes will be found in the Bibliography under the authors' names, except for *Bahá'í Holy Places*, *The Bahá'í World*, *Synopsis and Codification of the Laws and Ordinances of the Kitáb-i-Aqdas* and *Star of the West*, which are listed alphabetically by titles. Authors' names are not given in the Notes for three titles which are frequently mentioned; they are Balyuzi, *Bahá'u'lláh, The King of Glory*; Blomfield, *The Chosen Highway*; and Shoghi Effendi, *God Passes By*.

1. THE HOLY LAND

[1] In Genesis 49:20: 'Asher's food shall be rich, and he shall yield royal dainties.'

[2] In Genesis 49:13: 'Zebulun shall dwell at the shore of the sea; he shall become a haven for ships . . .'

[3] See the Qur'án, Súrih xvii: 'The Night Journey' (Rodwell translation, p. 164); the dream is said to have occurred one year before the Hijrah, in the twelfth year of the Prophet Muḥammad's Mission.

4. PILGRIMAGE TO THE HOLY LAND

[1] The Most Holy Shrine is the Tomb of Bahá'u'lláh at Bahjí, near 'Akká in Israel. To Bahá'ís it is the holiest Spot in the world, the Bahá'í Qiblih or point to which one turns in prayer.

6. THE PRISON CITY

The verses at the opening are by Rabbi Yehuda Alkharizi, Hatahmoni 47, AD 1216, translation by Dr Ze'ev Goldmann (from Dichter, *The Maps of Acre*).

[1] In Judges 1:31–2: 'Neither did Asher drive out the inhabitants of Accho, nor the inhabitants of Zidon . . . Achzib . . . Aphik. . . But the Asherites dwelt among the Canaanites, the inhabitants of the land . . .'

[2] A tell (or tel) is a mound or low hill which was once the site of an ancient town or village, usually of a number of successive settlements extending over centuries, the later buildings constructed upon the ruins of the earlier.

[3] In Acts of the Apostles 21:7: 'When we had finished the voyage from Tyre, we arrived at Ptolemais; and we greeted the brethren and stayed with them for one day.' Thus the New Testament records the visit of St. Paul to 'Akká in the Roman period.

7. THE ARRIVAL AND THE BARRACKS

[1] From the diary of Dr Ḥabíb Mu'ayyad (Khudábakhsh) comes the following information. During a walk through 'Akká with the Master, when passing the police station in the centre of the city, 'Abdu'l-Bahá recalled that first traverse from

the sea gate through hostile 'Akká to the station. 'They first wanted to confine us here, but we did not accept. Then they took us to the barracks.'

2 The construction of the principal mosque of the city was begun in 1781 by the governor, Aḥmad al-Jazzár, apparently upon the foundations of the Crusader Church of St. John in the northern part of the city close to the barracks and citadel.

3 In *Bahá'u'lláh, The King of Glory*, pp. 275–7, the barracks and prison are well described, as recalled by two of the exiles in their chronicles. The list of the exiles is given on pp. 277–9. The traditions and prophecies which were fulfilled with the arrival of the Great One are succinctly given on pp. 280–82. See also *God Passes By*, pp. 183–4.

4 As the prison complex now appears to visitors, Bahá'u'lláh's cell and the adjacent areas on the first floor of the north-western wing are as altered into a formal prison by the British Mandatory administration, which installed.prison ironwork, also to be seen on the ground floor. In recent years the Israeli Government has made the western half of the wing into a museum, while the eastern half was walled off for use by the mental hospital which was closed in 1980. Happily, since the 1920s the Mandate Government and the Government of Israel have recognized the cell as a Bahá'í Holy Place.

5 The Ḥammám al-Páshá, the Bath of al-Jazzár, has now been converted into the City Museum of 'Akká, a place where photographs, maps, and many artefacts of past centuries recreate a portion of the city's troubled history.

6 Badí' also means 'the new one', 'the one renewed', and certainly the youth became a new person through the power of Bahá'u'lláh.

8. THREE HOUSES IN THE WESTERN QUARTER

1 Mírzá Músá lived in the house of Malik for some time after his occupancy of the house within the courtyard of the Khán-i-'Avámíd. Thereafter Mírzá Muḥammad-Qulí with his family occupied the house of Malik, as later did his son 'Abdu'r-Ra'úf. Mírzá Músá lived also in a house overlooking the Khán-i-Shávirdí, at the edge of what is now Haim Farhí Square and was there visited by Bahá'u'lláh.

2 In later years the Khavvám family became enemies of the Faith; see *Bahá'u'lláh, The King of Glory*, pp. 364–5.

3 See Appendix II concerning the merchant 'Údí Khammár and his fateful association with the Faith.

9. THE HOUSE OF 'ÚDÍ KHAMMÁR

1 See *God Passes By*, p. 112, for a characterization of this 'black-hearted scoundrel' to whom Bahá'u'lláh referred as the one who had 'led astray' Mírzá Yaḥyá, and who was 'the source of envy and the quintessence of mischief'.

2 See *The Chosen Highway*, pp. 250–55 for further descriptions of the Azalí incident, the events surrounding the murders, the prison, etc. See also *Bahá'u'lláh, The King of Glory*, pp. 320–32.

3 In earlier days, Bahá'u'lláh had chosen His niece in Ṭihrán to be the wife of 'Abdu'l-Bahá, but obstacles were raised by His aunt, and she remained in Persia to become the bride of another. See *Bahá'u'lláh, The King of Glory*, pp. 342–4.

4 Muḥammad-Ḥasan and Muḥammad-Ḥusayn, sons of Mírzá Ibráhím, were martyred in Iṣfahán in 1878, and were then given the titles of the King and the Beloved of Martyrs by Bahá'u'lláh; they were cousins of Fáṭimih, Munírih Khánum.

5 An account of the marriage, by Munírih Khánum herself, is found in the booklet *Episodes in the Life of Moneereh Khanum*; extracts are retranslated by Mr Balyuzi in *Bahá'u'lláh, The King of Glory*, pp. 346–8.

6 *Synopsis and Codification of the Laws and Ordinances of the Kitáb-i-Aqdas* is a small book of 66 pages, concentrated in its subject-matter, its main sections revealing the scope of the topics covered, its notes helpfully amplifying many points. Passages

from the *Kitáb-i-Aqdas* selected and translated by Shoghi Effendi comprise pp. 11–28.

[7] Shaykh Maḥmúd 'Arrábí became a Bahá'í as a direct consequence of the interpretation of the 1850 phenomenon of a second sunset, by Shaykh Sa'íd al-Sa'dí for Shaykh Qásim 'Arrábí, the former a close friend of Shaykh Maḥmud's deceased father. See Appendix I for a detailed story of this remarkable man. See also *The Chosen Highway*, pp. 239–41.

[8] The photograph of Colonel Aḥmad Jarráḥ was hung in 1953 at the foot of the great stairs at Mazra'ih by the Guardian, who said that as he was the guard at the cell of Bahá'u'lláh, so let him be the guard here.

[9] The three sons of Dr Muḥammad Najím were Khálid, Amín and Aḥmad. Coming to the Holy Land as a military surgeon with the Egyptian forces of Ibráhím Páshá in 1831, Dr Najím married and lived in 'Akká after the Egyptian withdrawal in 1840. Khálid became a physician, and was Bahá'u'lláh's doctor at the time of His last illness; Amín became the mayor of 'Akká; Aḥmad became colonel of the guard. These sons accepted the Faith while Bahá'u'lláh lived in the House of 'Abbúd. 'Abdu'l-Raḥmán Jarráḥ, son of Aḥmad, was for a time custodian of the Mansion of Mazra'ih; he gave his one-fourth interest in the Garden of Junaynih to the Faith. (Jarráḥ means 'surgeon' in Arabic.)

10. THE HOUSE OF 'ABBÚD

[1] The house of Tannús Farráḥ was the site of the Master's *bírúní*, His reception room and consultation office. It fronts on Genoa Square, formerly known as 'Abbúd Square, diagonally opposite the House of 'Údí Khammár. The original house of the *bírúní* has been razed and a new building occupies the site.

[2] Ilyás 'Abbúd died in 1878 and is buried in a chamber across the street from the Church of St. George near his famous house; his tomb is marked by a special epitaph:

This is the tomb of 'Abbúd the sagacious!
Whose hands were ever engaged in deeds of generosity.
Thus Ilyás resembles his namesake Elijah in nobility,
That nobility which 'Akká, like a grateful singer, constantly praises.
He combined eminence with culture and practicality,
And built places of beauty and utility.
And yet he protected all who knocked at his door,
All who suffered the cruelty and violence of his time . . .

[3] The words quoted are from *God Passes By*, p. 216. See *Tablets of Bahá'u'lláh Revealed after the Kitáb-i-Aqdas* for a large selection of His Writings of that time. Over 15,000 of Bahá'u'lláh's Tablets, exclusive of His books, were held in 1982 at the World Centre.

[4] See Chapter 21, 'Water for 'Akká . . .', for details of the aqueduct construction and function.

11. 'ABDU'L-BAHÁ IN 'AKKÁ: 1877–1892

[1] 'Ayn is the first letter of his Father's name, 'Abbás.

[2] A reference to Qur'án xviii: 46 ('The Cave'). In the Rodwell translation, p. 184.

[3] In the original Persian Bahá'u'lláh makes a fond play on the word 'tamáshá' which means 'sightseeing', a word which the little child mispronounced as 'tabáshá' which has no meaning. Thus in the inscription: '. . . instead of "tabáshá" we see him now engaged in "tamáshá" in the heavenly realms.'

[4] The Persian title of *The Secret of Divine Civilization*, published originally as the *Mysterious Forces of Civilization*, is *Risáliy-i-Madaníyyih* (literally, 'A Treatise on Civilization').

[5] By 1982 the number of Tablets known to have emanated from the pen of the

Master, and now in the international archives at the World Centre, exceeded 26,000.

12.   THE HOUSE OF 'ABDU'LLÁH PÁSHÁ

[1] The great complex which became the Governorate of 'Abdu'lláh Páshá was built by his father 'Alí Páshá, *c.* 1810. See Appendix III, and its Note 1.

[2] The governor removed by the Commission of Inquiry was Ibráhím Sarím Bey (1905). See Momen, *The Bábí and Bahá'í Religions* pp. 320–23, for an account, from official sources, of the Commission's activities and the discrepancy in dates of its arrival.

[3] The Commission of Inquiry lived in the Baydún Mansion, on the invitation of 'Abdu'l-Ghaní Baydún to be his guests. The Muslim Baydúns were consistent enemies of the Faith.

13.   THE KHÁN-I-'AVÁMÍD: THE FIRST PILGRIM HOUSE

[1] A valuable description of the Khán-i-'Avámíd is found in *The Chosen Highway*, pp. 230–31.

15.   BAHÁ'Í CEMETERIES IN 'AKKÁ

[1] The Nabí Sálih, patron saint of 'Akká, after whom the cemetery is named, is unlikely to be the Sálih mentioned by Muhammad in the Qur'án vii. 71–7, 'Al-Araf' (Sura lxxxvii in Rodwell's translation), revealed in Mecca. Sálih was an Arabian prophet who followed Noah and Húd in the Qur'anic ordering. In the *Kitáb-i-Íqán*, p. 9, Bahá'u'lláh refers to Sálih and his hundred years of mission, but nowhere later connects the prophet with the holy man of 'Akká, whoever he may have been.

16.   MAZRA'IH: PLACE OF LIBERATION

[1] Muhammad Páshá Safwat was the grandnephew of 'Abdu'lláh Páshá (governor from 1819 to 1832), i.e. the grandson of 'Abdu'lláh's sister Miriam. At this time he may have been living in the great complex later to be rented to 'Abdu'l-Bahá in 1896, or perhaps at what is now called the Baydún mansion. The house at Mazra'ih, built at a spot called Alexandrona in pre-Ottoman times, had been constructed before AD 1800. Its former owners were Yúsuf Máwí, then 'Abdu'l-Qádir al-Sammáwí, then 'Alí Páshá, father of 'Abdu'lláh, who passed it to his son. It is not known precisely when the changes and additions to the Mansion occurred, but they are visibly many and extensive.

[2] The Mansion (Qasr) was located across a valley from the village of Mazra'ih (literally, 'the farm').

[3] The Muslim notable involved in this touching incident was Shaykh 'Alíy-i-Mírí who was then, or soon became, the Muftí of 'Akká. His home adjoined the House of 'Abdu'lláh Páshá in the Mujádalih Quarter and was attached to it at its southern wall by a heavy arch spanning the roadway. It is recorded that, in the latter years of the Master's sojourn in the prison city, He, 'in the winter season . . . met with the learned and notables of 'Akká at the home of [the great master] Sheikh Ali Meeri [may God illumine his resting-place!] . . .' At that resting-place his daughter Khadíjih's tombstone carries a poetic tribute to '. . . 'Alí Effendi, the Muftí of 'Akká, who combined nobility with generosity, and whose long life was filled with bounties and glory . . .' (The words quoted in lines 5–7 come from *Star of the West*, vol. xii, no. 17, p. 266; those in brackets within these lines appear in an Arabic extract on p. 284 from the Egyptian Arabic newspaper *Annafír*, December 1921.)

[4] According to Nabíl's documentation, Bahá'u'lláh's transfer to Mazra'ih occurred some time between 3 and 10 June 1877. At present it seems impossible to fix a precise date.

⁵ The aqueduct from the Kabrí springs to 'Akká runs across the Mazra'ih property from north to south, thus once providing an ample water-supply for the house, gardens and fields.

⁶ Many of Ḥájí Muḥammad-Ṭáhir's unique experiences are recorded in the books of his son Adib Taherzadeh (now a member of the Board of Counsellors), entitled *The Revelation of Bahá'u'lláh*, vols. 1 and 2.

⁷ Ḥájí Mullá Mihdíy-i-Yazdí was the father of the Hand of the Cause Valíyu'lláh Varqá, and grandfather of the present Hand of the Cause 'Alí-Muḥammad Varqá.

⁸ The epidemic seems likely to have been bubonic plague, since that well-known disease was a frequent visitor to the rat-infested port city of 'Akká, and the word itself is used in the reports.

⁹ Mrs McNeill has written that she and Queen Marie 'became acquainted [with the Bahá'í Faith] about the same time, she in Rumania, I in Palestine'. (See McNeill in Bibliography.) Mrs McNeill is interred in the Commonwealth Cemetery in Haifa.

17. THE RIDVÁN GARDEN

¹ The name of the little river Na'mayn means 'two yeses' in Arabic. There is a tradition in Islám that on the Last Day, in response to the Divine Call 'Am I not your Lord?', two yeses will be heard. There are other explanatory traditions as well.

² The early seafaring Greek traders had, by at least the thirteenth century BC, named the peoples of Syrian–Palestinian Canaan 'Phoenicians' and their country 'Phoenicia'. The Greek word 'Phoenikos' was almost a direct translation of the name 'Canaan', which means 'land of purple', i.e. land of the purple-dye industry, for already in those long-ago centuries the Canaanites of the Palestinian coast were famous for the dye which they produced from Murex species of sea snails.

18. BAHJÍ: DAYS OF GLORY AND REVELATION

¹ When Bahá'u'lláh lived in the Mansion of Bahjí its neighbouring mansion to the south (of the Páshás Sulaymán and 'Abdu'lláh) was occupied by the then friendly Christian Jamál brothers, Jirjis (Georges) and Iskandar (Alexander), who later became hostile to 'Abdu'l-Bahá. Thereafter it was purchased by the unfriendly Muslim Baydúns. After their flight in 1948 it became an Israeli institution for boys, the Atidot School.

² The source of the remarkable passage over the doorway is not known, if indeed it is a quotation; it may derive from an obscure writer, or be 'Údí Khammár's own composition.

³ Among sources rich in material on Bahá'u'lláh's Bahjí period are 'Abdu'l-Bahá's *Memorials of the Faithful, God Passes By, Bahá'u'lláh, The King of Glory* and *The Chosen Highway*.

⁴ A brief biography of Ḥájí Mullá 'Alí-Akbar is found in the Master's book, *Memorials of the Faithful*, pp. 9–12.

⁵ The nature of Bahá'u'lláh's final sickness was said to be malaria (see *The Chosen Highway*, p. 105); in view of the endemic malaria of the 'Akká district this is possible, but seems unlikely from the descriptions available. Dr Khálid Jarráḥ attended Bahá'u'lláh in His last illness.

⁶ Bahá'u'lláh's son-in-law was Siyyid 'Alí Afnán, husband of Furúghíyyih Khánum; both became Covenant-breakers. See Balyuzi, *Khadíjih Bagum*, for an account of Siyyid 'Alí Afnán's disgraceful treatment of and broken promises to the wife of the Báb.

⁷ For an account of the passing of Bahá'u'lláh see also that of Ṭúbá Khánum, daughter of 'Abdu'l-Bahá, in *The Chosen Highway*, pp. 105–9.

19. BAHJÍ: DAYS OF SORROW AND REGENERATION

¹ What is now known as the Tea House of 'Abdu'l-Bahá is a three-room, single-storey structure just outside the northern wall of the Baydún estate, at the southern

225

edge of the Bahá'í property. It was owned by a Persian family loyal to the Master, and some years ago was converted by the Guardian to its present state, its roof-top structures and staircase having been removed.

[2] About 1892 the Master rented the house which is now known as the Pilgrim House at Bahjí from its Christian owner, Iskandar Ḥawwá', husband of 'Údí Khammár's daughter Haní. Salím Ḥawwá', son of Iskandar, fled from Israel in 1948. The property was acquired about 1956 from the Israeli Government as part of the exchange for the Ein Gev properties. See Appendix IV and Shoghi Effendi, *Messages to the Bahá'í World*, pp. 45–6.

[3] Muhammad-'Alí, half-brother of 'Abdu'l-Bahá and arch-Covenant-breaker, died on 20 December 1937; a cablegram of that date from Shoghi Effendi recorded his passing.

[4] The houses surrounding the Mansion of Bahjí were built by Iskandar Ḥawwá', husband of 'Údí Khammár's daughter, and were used by the families related to them for summer occupancy and events such as feasts.

20. OTHER SITES RELATED TO THE FAITH IN THE ENVIRONS OF 'AKKÁ

[1] Israel is famed for its red wild-flowers, among which is the turban buttercup, *Ranunculus asiaticus*, which produces a cluster of large scarlet blooms. There are also local species of typical yellow buttercups.

21. WATER FOR 'AKKÁ: THE SPRINGS AND THE AQUEDUCT

[1] The Spring of the Cow is named from the Muslim legend that Adam watered his ox here; hence among other ascriptions the spring water is thought to be healing to oxen.

[2] The three springs of Kabrí have names dating from Arab times: 'Aynu'l-Báshá, number one near Kibbutz Kabrí; 'Aynu'l-'Asal, number two; and 'Aynu'l-Favvár, number three near Tell Naḥaf and the former Garden of 'Afífí.

23. THE SHRINE OF THE BÁB

[1] For details of the building of the superstructure see *The Bahá'í World*, vol. xii, pp. 238–52, and Giachery, *Shoghi Effendi*, pp. 68–108.

[2] The Master named the five doors of the original Shrine with its six chambers after five disciples: Báb-i-Amín, for Ḥájí Amín, and Báb-i-Bálá, for Ustád Áqá Bálá, for the two doors of the outer rooms opening upon the Tomb of the Báb itself; Báb-i-Faḍl and Báb-i-Ashraf, for Mírzá Abu'l-Faḍl of Gulpáygán and Ustád Áqá 'Alí-Ashraf; and Báb-i-Karím, for Ustád 'Abdu'l-Karím – these for the three outer doors of the Tomb of the Master. For an exposition of the naming of all doors of the Shrine see Giachery, *Shoghi Effendi*, pp. 214–16. (See also Chap. 17 describing the Ashraf Garden.)

24. THE HOUSE OF THE MASTER

[1] This panelled room served the Hands of the Cause as an office during the period from 1957 to 1963, and for some years thereafter. (The description is from *Bahá'í Holy Places*, p. 56.)

[2] This summary of 'Abdu'l-Bahá's passing derives from 'An Account of the Passing of 'Abdu'l-Bahá' in *The Bahá'í World*, vol. xv, pp. 113–24, which includes tributes to the Master at His funeral and memorial feast as well as extracts from newspapers and cablegrams. Balyuzi, *'Abdu'l-Bahá*, Chap. 24, is a similar rich source of information.

27. THE MONUMENT GARDENS

[1] In Rabbani, *The Priceless Pearl*, pp. 259–63, is a moving and graphic description of

the events associated with the exhumation, transfer and reburial of the remains of the mother and brother of the Master. See also her article in *The Bahá'í World*, vol. viii, pp. 253–8.

28. THE INTERNATIONAL BAHÁ'Í ARCHIVES

[1] The construction and furnishing of the International Archives building has been movingly and exhaustively treated by Amatu'l-Bahá Rúḥíyyih Khánum in *The Bahá'í World*, vol. xiii, pp. 403–33.

29. THE ARC AND THE WORLD ADMINISTRATIVE CENTRE

[1] See *The Bahá'í World*, vol. xvi, pp. 399–404, for an illuminating article on the Seat of The Universal House of Justice by its architect, Mr Ḥusayn Amánat.

30. THE SITE OF THE MASHRIQU'L-ADHKÁR IN HAIFA

[1] The account of the revelation of the *Tablet of Carmel* derives from an onlooker, Ḥusayn Iqbál of the local Bahá'í community. Other words quoted in paragraph 2 are from *God Passes By*, p. 194.

[2] The name 'Ladder of Tyre' is given to the several long east–west-trending parallel mountains which run to the sea between the ancient cities of Achziv and Tyre.

31. THE PILGRIM HOUSE IN HAIFA

[1] Mírzá Ja'far Raḥmání was born in 'Ishqábád in Turkistan (now Soviet Turkmenistan), and had lived in Shíráz before settling in Iṣfahán. His son Hádí Raḥmání of Ṭihrán is a distinguished servant of the Faith.

34. THE CAVES OF ELIJAH ON MOUNT CARMEL

[1] The prophet Elijah (lit., 'Jehovah is my God') lived in the middle of the ninth century BC, in the northern kingdom of Israel during the reign of Ahab and his successor, Ahaziah. Challenging the priests of the Canaanite gods brought by Jezebel the queen, he fought to maintain the integrity of monotheistic Judaism.

[2] See *The Chosen Highway*, p. 199.

35. THE SOCIETY OF THE TEMPLE

[1] In *Ephesians* 2:19–20 St. Paul states: 'Now therefore ye are no more strangers and foreigners, but fellow-citizens with the saints, and of the household of God; And are built upon the foundation of the apostles and prophets, Jesus Christ himself being the chief corner stone . . .'

[2] In *I Peter* 2:5 St. Peter says: 'Ye also, as lively stones, are built up a spiritual house, an holy priesthood, to offer up spiritual sacrifices, acceptable to God by Jesus Christ.'

[3] The material on the Templers derives principally from the commemorative Templer brochure by Dr Richard Otto Hoffmann, 1 May 1974, entitled 'In Memory of Those Who Have Gone before Us'. It is plain that original Templer ideas have undergone modification with time and dimming of the Adventist expectations.

[4] The German spelling 'Templer', as in the literature of the Society of the Temple itself, is used throughout, partly to avoid confusion with the Crusader Knights of the Temple, the Templars.

[5] In the house with the prophetic inscription 'Der Herr ist nahe' a little girl was born, probably in 1887, her name Wilhelmine Pfander; she married to become Mrs Deininger. In 1977 the wife of Gerhard Schmelzle, a Templer born in Haifa who had gone to Australia with his parents and had there become a Bahá'í in his maturity, sought Mrs Deininger at her home in South Australia and inquired about her childhood in that house. The aged woman clearly recalled the tent on the open land next door, that Holy Place which is now marked by a circle of cypresses.

While Bahá'u'lláh and His companions were there, when she was 'four or five', she recounted, He had had a brief illness and had been invited into the Pfander home for a time while He was seen by the Templer doctor, possibly Dr J. Schmidt. She recalled having seen Bahá'u'lláh in the room at the north-west corner of the ground floor.

APPENDICES

II. THE MERCHANT 'ÚDÍ KHAMMÁR

[1] There are perhaps 500 Christian Arabs now living in the walled city.

[2] Malik may have been a member of the Khammár family, for in one of the receipts for rents paid by 'Abdu'l-Bahá he signs his name 'Khammár'.

[3] Important links between the Khammár family and 'Abbúd existed: 'Abbúd's daughter married Ilyás Khammár, 'Údí Khammár's brother, and their daughter married Andrávís, son of 'Údí Khammár. Both families were wealthy in Bahá'u'lláh's time, and supported the restorations in the Church of St. George, contributing new items for its beautification. Nearby present-day Genoa Square was then named 'Abbúd Square.

III. THE LIFE OF 'ABDU'LLÁH PÁSHÁ

[1] A document of 1812 details the waqf holdings of 'Alí Páshá (titled Emir in some records), father of 'Abdu'lláh Páshá and associate of fellow Mameluke Sulaymán Páshá. It includes descriptions of the great complex inside the walled city which became his son's Governorate, the khán which he built now called the barracks, the stables south of Sulaymán's mansion now the agricultural school, and Mazra'ih with its orchards.

[2] The British war fleet unit was under the command of Admiral Sir Robert Stopford.

IV. BAHÁ'Í PROPERTIES IN THE GALILEE AND JORDAN VALLEY

[1] In *The Chosen Highway*, pp. 209–10, is a useful summary of the Bahá'í settlements beside or in the vicinity of the Sea of Galilee.

[2] Two sons of Mírzá Muḥammad-Qulí, Munír and 'Abdu'r-Ra'úf, were buried in Tiberias, while Mírzá Muḥammad-Qulí, his two wives, his third son Dhikru'lláh and nine relatives are buried at Nuqayb/Ein Gev. These thirteen soon will be reinterred at a nearby site at the foot of the Golan escarpment, below the ancient tell of the city of Hippos/Susita.

V. THE DRUZE OF ISRAEL

[1] Some historians have supposed that the disappearance of the Caliph al-Ḥákim was in fact a murder by his aggrieved sister, his body being secretly disposed of.

[2] Much additional information on the doctrines and history of the Druze is contained in the *Encyclopaedia of Islam*, vol. II (authors Hodgson, Tekindag, Gökbilgin), 1965, new edn, and in the *Encyclopaedia Britannica*, vol. 5 (author Hirschberg), 1976, 15th edn. There is also a brief description of the Druze attributed to 'Abdu'l-Bahá in *The Chosen Highway*, p. 195, and a long description by Rúḥá Khánum of a visit to Abú-Sinán, on pp. 198–200.

Index

Entries are alphabetized by word; component parts of hyphenated names are treated as separate words, but the connective -i- is ignored. Thus, 'Alíy-i- is treated as if it were spelt 'Alí. Similarly, only major words are alphabetized, so that *Bahá'u'lláh, The King of Glory* precedes *Bahá'u'lláh and the New Era*. The prefix al- is ignored for purposes of indexing. Members of Bahá'u'lláh's Family appear under their titles, e.g. the Greatest Holy Leaf, rather than their given names, although they are cross-referenced.

'Akká (Accho, Accon, Acre, Akko, Ptolemais), illustrations, 10–11, 18, 19, 21, 22–3, 25, 26–7, 27, 37, 82, 83, 126–7, 184; 2, 9, 100, 133, 197, 200, 221, 222, 224

'Abdu'l-Bahá
  feeds population of, in World War One, 209
  prepares pilgrims to meet Bahá'u'lláh, 107
  reincarceration, 67–8
  remains in, 147
  services to needy of, 56, 68
  vision of Haifa and 'Akká, 21
  visited by Shaykh Yúsuf in, 57
  visits, 79
Akko (Biblical), 17, 22
Alkharizi's poem about, 22
ancient, 2
aqueduct to, q.v.
Arab port, 126
area assigned to Tribe of Asher, 8
arrival at,
  described by Bahá'u'lláh, 28
  described by Greatest Holy Leaf, 26
Bahá'í property in, exempt from taxes, 120
and Bahá'u'lláh
  allowed to leave, 54, 88–9, 95, 213
  arrival in, 11, 12, 24, 198
  banishment to, 10
  description of arrival in, 26, 28
  influence on 'Akká, 53
  visits, while at Mazra'ih, 90
barracks of, q.v.
bequest of believers in, 122
Britain regains, for Turkey, 206
British officer in, 116
Carmel Avenue points to, 154
changes in, 43–4
children of, 76
Christian denominations in, 201, 228
Commission (of Inquiry) in, 69–71
  ship waits for 'Abdu'l-Bahá in, 70
Crusader capital, 24
decline of, 21, 24
defence of road into, 79
description of, 2
designated 'Most Great Prison', 53
Egyptians attack, 24, 206
environs of, 123–4
exiles in, 222
  population ill-disposed to, 43
fall of, 19
geography of, 125–6
governor of, 42, 43, 63, 67
  dismissed by Commission, 70
Greatest Holy Leaf describes arrival at, 26
and Haifa
  communication with, 133
  to fuse together, 73

links prophesied, 135–6
history of, 17–21, 22–4
  scriptural, 22
holy city for Bahá'í Faith, 21
Holy Family moved from, 145
houses in Western Quarter of, 38–9
inhabitants of,
  provocative behaviour of, 68
  ill-disposed towards exiles, 43
kháns of, q.v.
land gate of, see Gates
malaria in, 225
mayor of (Amín Jarráh), 223
'metropolis of the owl', 24, 134
Mírzá 'Abdu'l-Ahad sent to, 32
Mírzá Músá's passing in, 57, 213
Monument Gardens face, 163
Muhammad Páshá Safwat must live in, 87
Mujádalih Quarter in, q.v.
Munírih Khánum arrives in, 45
'museum city', 17–21
museum for Bahá'ís, 73
Nabí Sálih patron saint of, 81
Navváb's passing in, 57, 213
  interred in cemetery at, 57, 81, 162
no carriages in, 87
pilgrims to, 3, 13, 32–5, 100, 200
  arrival reported by Azalís, 46
  forbidden entry by firman, 49, 52
  and land gate, 79
plague in, 91, 203, 225
police station at, illustration, 27; 26, 221–2
'prison-city', 22–5
Ptolemais (Roman), 17
remains of the Báb arrive in, 66, 214
St. Paul's visit to, 221
sea gate of, see Gates
Shoghi Effendi born in, 60, 73
Shrine of the Báb faces, 139
site of Turkish military activity, 37
size of Crusader city, 18
springs near, see Springs
and Sulaymán Páshá, 20, 127, 205
telegraph and postal services in, 70
Tell of, see 'Akká, Tell
traditions relating to, 22–3, 49, 222
visitors to, blessed, 22–3
water for, 125–9, see also Aqueduct and Springs
World War One in, 147, 179, 209
Záhiru'l-'Umar rebuilds, 20
'Akká, Tell (Hill of the Shards, Napoleon's Hill, Tell al-Fakhkhár), illustration, 20–21, 125
Accho situated at, 22, 101
Bahá'u'lláh pitched tent at, 17, 124
Bahá'u'lláh visits, 108
dig at, 2
names of, 17
Ridván Garden near, 95
Akko, see 'Akká
'Akko, new, Jewish 'Akká, 21

Aleppo, 10
Alexander the Great, 23
Alexandria, 11, 45
Alexandrona, 224
'Alí Afnán, Siyyid, 225
'Alí-Akbar-i-Shahmírzádí, Hájí Mullá (Hájí Ákhúnd), Hand of the Cause, 109, 225
'Alí-Ashraf, 104, 226
  garden of, see Ashraf Garden
'Alíy-i-Mírí, Shaykh (Muftí of 'Akká, illustration, 83; 224
  persuades Bahá'u'lláh to go to Mazra'ih, 49–50, 87–8
'Alí-Muhammad, Mírzá (Ibn-i-Asdaq), Hand of the Cause, 109
'Alí Páshá, 30, 205, 224, 228
  khán of, illustration, 28–9
Alkharizi, Rabbi Yehuda
  poem about 'Akká, 22, 221
Alláh-u-Abhá, 198–9
Allenby, General, 91, 149
Allenby Road, 181, 186
Alms, 49, 64, 68, 75
Amalfi, 19
Amánat, Husayn, 172, 227
Amatu'l-Bahá Rúhíyyih Khánum (Rabbani), 140, 215, 226, 227
  describes childhood of Shoghi Effendi, 61
  describes death of Purest Branch, 36
  furnishes International Bahá'í Archives building, 169, 227
  and house of the Master, 152
  marriage of, 152, 215
American University of Beirut (Syrian Protestant College), 148, 214
Amín-i-Iláhí (Hájí Amín, Hájí Abu'l-Hasan-i-Ardikání), Hand of the Cause, 33–4, 226
  Bahá'u'lláh's Tablet to, 33–4
Amos, 7–8
An-Nahr, 123, 128
Ancona, 19
Annafir, 224
Aphek, 221
Áqá 'Alí-Ashraf, Ustád, 226
Áqá Bálá, Ustád, 226
Áqá Ján, Mírzá, Khádimu'lláh, 89, 107, 203
Áqá Ján Big-i-Kaj-Kuláh, 40–41
Áqáy-i-Kalím, see Músá, Áqáy-i-Kalím, Mírzá
al-Aqsá, Mosque of, 8
Aqueduct, illustrations, 89, 104–5, 126–7, 129; 126–9, 205
  ancient, 126–7
  Bahá'u'lláh requests Ahmad Big Tawfíq to repair, 52
  construction of, 223
  course of, 107, 127, 225
  destroyed by Napoleon, 20, 127
  first, constructed by al-Jazzár, 20, 127

231

242